IMPACT
CALIFORNIA SOCIAL STUDIES

Continuity and Change

LANGUAGE LEARNERS TEACHING GUIDE
GRADE 3

McGraw Hill Education

Program Authors

James Banks, Ph.D.
Kerry and Linda Killinger
Endowed Chair in Diversity
Studies and Director, Center
for Multicultural Education
University of Washington
Seattle, Washington

Kevin P. Colleary
Curriculum and Teaching
Department Graduate School
of Education
Fordham University
New York, New York

Willam Deverell, Ph.D.
Director of the Huntington-
USC Institute on California
and the West, Professor of
History, University of
Southern California
Los Angeles, California

Daniel Lewis, Ph.D.
Dibner Senior Curator
The Huntington Library
Los Angeles, California

Elizabeth Lewis Ph.D., J.D.
Associate Director of the
Huntington-USC Institute
on California and the West
Los Angeles, California

Walter C. Parker, Ph.D.
Professor of Social Studies
Education and Adjunct Professor
of Political Science
University of Washington
Seattle, Washington

Emily M. Schell, Ed.D.
Professor, Teacher Education
San Diego State University
San Diego, California

Program Consultants

Jana Echevarria, Ph.D.
Professor Emerita
California State University
Long Beach, California

Douglas Fisher, Ph.D.
Professor, Educational Leadership
San Diego State University
San Diego, California

Jay McTighe
Jay McTighe and Associates

Rebecca Valbuena
K-5 Teacher on Special
Assignment/Academic Coach
Glendora Unified School District
Glendora, California

Carlos Ulloa, Ed.D
Principal, Escondido Union
School District
Escondido, California

Program Reviewers

Nafees Khan, Ph.D.
Department of Teaching
and Learning
Social Studies Education
Clemson University
Clemson, South Carolina

Lorri Glover, Ph.D
John Francis Bannon, S.J.
Professor of History
Saint Louis University
St. Louis, Missouri

Gary Clayton, Ph.D.
Professor of Economics
Northern Kentucky University
Highland Heights, Kentucky

Thomas Herman, Ph.D.
Distinguished Professor of History
Rupert Costo Chair in American
Indian Affairs
University of California
Riverside, California

mheducation.com/prek-12

Copyright © 2019 McGraw-Hill Education

All rights reserved. No part of this publication may be
reproduced or distributed in any form or by any means,
or stored in a database or retrieval system, without the
prior written consent of McGraw-Hill Education,
including, but not limited to, network storage or
transmission, or broadcast for distance learning.

Send all inquiries to:
McGraw-Hill Education
303 East Wacker Drive, Suite 2000
Chicago, IL 60601

ISBN: 978-0-07-899384-8
MHID: 0-07-899384-9

Printed in the United States of America.

2 3 4 5 6 WEB 21 20 19 18 17

OPPOSITE:(l to r) Edward S. Curtis Collection, Library of Congress, LC-USZ62-118769, Ron and Patty Thomas Photography/E+/Getty Images, Mitch Diamond/Photodisc/Getty Images, netopaek/iStockphoto/Getty Images

Welcome to
IMPACT
CALIFORNIA SOCIAL STUDIES
Language Learners Teaching Guide

Language Learners Teaching Guide

The *California IMPACT Social Studies Language Learners Teaching Guide* provides a focused language study designed to support language learners and help them gain content knowledge in the complex literacy-based History/Social Science discipline. The instructional model respects knowledge development as a process focused on growth, not mastery.

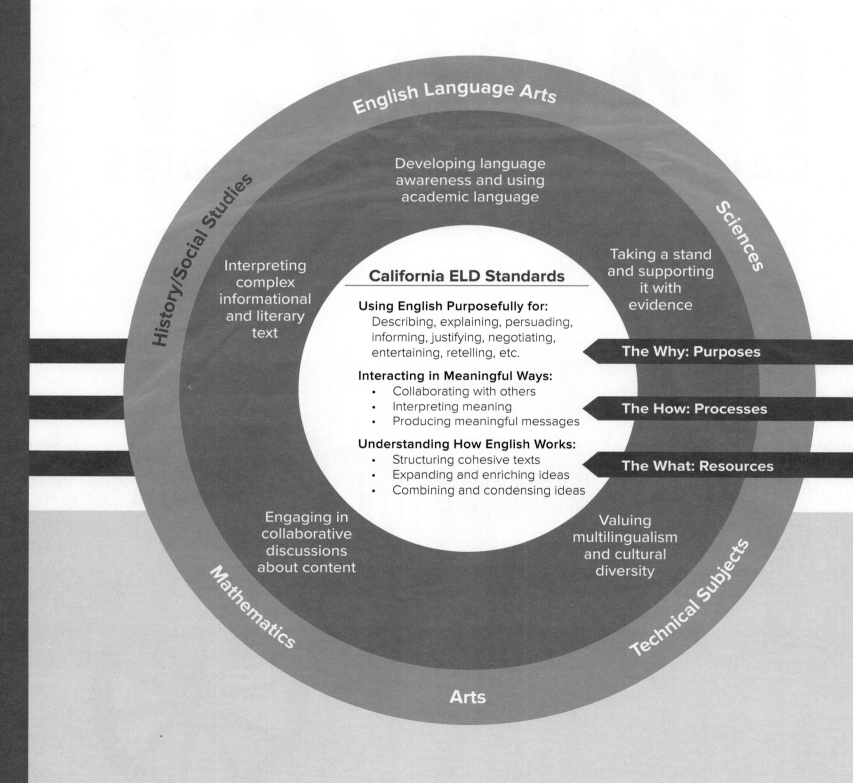

English Language Arts

History/Social Studies

Sciences

Developing language awareness and using academic language

Interpreting complex informational and literary text

Taking a stand and supporting it with evidence

California ELD Standards

Using English Purposefully for:
Describing, explaining, persuading, informing, justifying, negotiating, entertaining, retelling, etc.

Interacting in Meaningful Ways:
- Collaborating with others
- Interpreting meaning
- Producing meaningful messages

Understanding How English Works:
- Structuring cohesive texts
- Expanding and enriching ideas
- Combining and condensing ideas

The Why: Purposes

The How: Processes

The What: Resources

Engaging in collaborative discussions about content

Valuing multilingualism and cultural diversity

Mathematics

Technical Subjects

Arts

Table of Contents

Reference Section

CHAPTER 1 Communities in California

 How does geography impact California communities?

CHAPTER 2 American Indians of the Local Region

 How have California Indians influenced the local region?

CHAPTER 3 How and Why Communities Changed Over Time

 How has life changed for people in my community over time?

CHAPTER 4 American Citizens, Symbols, and Government

 How do our government and its citizens work together?

CHAPTER 5 Economics of the Local Region

 How do people in a community meet their needs?

McGraw-Hill Education's Guiding Principles for Supporting English Learners

McGraw-Hill Education is committed to providing English Learners appropriate support as they simultaneously learn content and language. As an organization, we recognize that the United States is a culturally and linguistically diverse country. Moreover, this diversity continues to increase, with corresponding growth in the number of English Learners (ELs). In 2012–2013, an estimated 4.85 million ELs were enrolled US schools; this subgroup now makes up nearly 10% of the total public school enrollment (Ruiz-Soto, Hooker, and Batalova, 2015). In fact, ELs are the fastest growing student population in the country, growing 60% in the last decade, compared with only 7% growth of the general student population (Grantmakers for Education, 2013). Perhaps most interesting of all, the vast majority of ELs—85% of prekindergarten through fifth grade ELs, and 62% of high school ELs—were born in the United States (Zong & Batalova, 2015). These US-born ELs may be first-, second-, or third-generation students with strong ties to their cultural roots.

A great many ELs come to school with a variety of rich linguistic and cultural backgrounds from Spanish-speaking communities and countries throughout the Americas. In addition to Spanish, there are some ELs that come to school speaking fluent or limited Spanish in addition to an indigenous language native to North, Central, and South America. In addition, schools experience native speakers from numerous other backgrounds and languages—the most common other languages being Cantonese, Hmong, Korean, Vietnamese, and Haitian Creole. While over 70% of ELs come to school speaking Spanish as their native language, as a group, ELs speak nearly 150 languages (Baird, 2015). The experiences and identities acquired in the context of ELs' homes and communities can transform the simplest classroom into a unique cultural and linguistic microcosm.

English Learners' success in learning a second language is influenced by a variety of factors besides the instructional method itself, including individual, family, and classroom characteristics; school and community contexts; the attributes of the assessment used to measure progress; and whether the language acquired is a national or foreign language (August & Shanahan, 2006; Genesee, Lindholm-Leary, Saundes, & Christian, 2006). For instance, children's initial levels of proficiency in their home language(s), along with English, influence new language acquisition (August, Shanahan, Escamilla, K., 2009) as does the quality of school support (Niehaus & Adelson, 2014) and the characteristics of the language learners' first and second languages (Dressler & Kamil, 2006)

Given these factors, there is a pressing need for fundamental principles that guide the support of ELs as they acquire content and develop language. Drawing upon extensive research in the field, McGraw-Hill Education has developed nine guiding principles for supporting English Learners at all grade levels and in all disciplines.

michaeljung/Shutterstock.com

Guiding Principles

- ✔ Provide Specialized Instruction

- ✔ Cultivate Meaning

- ✔ Teach Structure and Form

- ✔ Develop Language in Context

- ✔ Scaffold to Support Access

- ✔ Foster Interaction

- ✔ Create Affirming Cultural Spaces

- ✔ Engage Home to Enrich Instruction

- ✔ Promote Multilingualism

Cultivate Meaning and Support Language

Research shows that ELs are more motivated to learn English when they are integrated in the classroom, interacting with their English-speaking teachers and classmates, and receiving and producing English during their regular classes. ELs greatly benefit from the opportunity to regularly hear and speak English with their teachers and classmates. ELs learn faster in intellectually challenging classes with meaningful content, engaging activities, and quality instruction. However, research also shows that integrated instruction by itself is not always sufficient, and therefore designated support separate from mainstream classroom instruction is often necessary.

California IMPACT Language Learners Teaching Guide

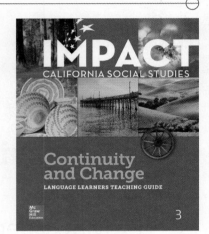

The **California IMPACT Language Learners Teaching Guide** provides the designated support designed for use outside of the mainstream classroom.

The Language Learners Teaching Guide provides instruction at three language proficiency levels with:

- Language and content objectives in every lesson;

- Core content as the vehicle to learning how English works;

- Gradual release of responsibility to the students accelerate progress;

- Frequent opportunities for English learners to collaborate, integrate ideas, and produce language.

The key is engagement. Research shows that children learn best when they are engaged with whatever it is they are learning about. Making activities relevant to children's daily lives is important, too, as is activating what they might already know from their life experiences thus far.

The **Designated** activities are:

- **language-focused** — to enable ELs to access language and concepts that prevent them from comprehending the core history-social science core content. They must also develop **register awareness** so that they understand how and when to use different types of English (everyday vs. academic, formal vs. informal; oral vs. written).

- **challenging** — students are encouraged to think critically about and analyze information themselves

- **productive** — ELs are asked to **produce** English (write or speak), as well as receive it (read or listen)

- **collaborative** — with lots of opportunities to work in pairs or small groups (with students of different proficiency levels), practicing all four skills.

- **engaging** — activities are student-friendly to **engage** ELs in the topic or activity presented in the student texts, make them **curious to find out more**, and enable them to **express their creativity**. ALL the research shows that children learn best when they are engaged with whatever it is they are learning about (true for adults too!). Making activities relevant to students' daily lives is important, too, as is connecting to what they might already know in their life experience thus far.

Inquiry Journal and Research Companion

Accelerate English language development by building content knowledge and supporting domain-specific language, tied to the core History/Social Science curriculum.

- Ensure equity of access to core content.
- Collaborate through speaking listening, reading, and writing.
- Prepare English learners for success on assessments.

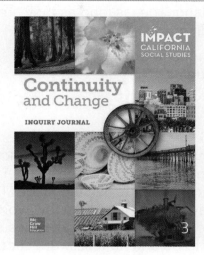

Teacher's Edition

The purpose of the English Learners Scaffold in the Teacher's Edition is to "unlock" language or concepts that prevent ELs from comprehending text and participating in classroom discussions and activities. ELs must learn to use and practice English in meaningful and authentic ways, and develop register awareness so that they understand how and when to use different types of English (formal vs. informal; oral vs. written).

The **Integrated** activities are:

- **leveled** — according to the three proficiency levels: emerging, expanding, and bridging
- **focused** — on one aspect in the student text spread that presents a specific challenge to ELs due to academic language or a challenging concept
- **productive** — students are urged to produce English, either written or oral, rather than simply receive it
- **collaborative** — with abundant opportunities for students of various proficiency levels to work in pairs or small groups.

Language Proficiency Level Descriptors

Research shows that English Learners at all proficiency levels are capable of high-level thinking and can engage in complex, cognitively demanding social and academic activities requiring language, as long as they are provided appropriate linguistic support and scaffolding.

The three levels of English language proficiency in *California IMPACT Social Studies* are:

EMERGING

These students might be newcomers with little knowledge of or exposure to English beyond answering simple questions. They will have varying degrees of proficiency in their native language. They need a HIGH level of support. Some may be able to write a few words; others may be unfamiliar with Western script. They might lack sufficient vocabulary and oral comprehension to be able to follow directions or classroom activities. However, they typically progress very quickly, learning to use English for immediate needs as well as beginning to understand and use academic language.

EXPANDING

These students are typically comfortable responding orally in the classroom, despite frequent errors and incorrect word usage. They need a MEDIUM level of support, and will exhibit growing confidence in their ability to comprehend and respond in English. Students at this level are challenged to increase their English skills in more contexts and learn a greater variety of vocabulary and linguistic structures, applying their growing language skills in more sophisticated ways that are appropriate to their age and grade level.

BRIDGING

Students at this level continue to learn and apply a range of high-level English language skills in a wide variety of contexts, including comprehension and production of highly technical texts. They require a LOW level of support. The "bridge" alluded to is the transition to full engagement in grade-level academic tasks and activities in a variety of content areas without the need for specialized ELD instruction.

Collaborative Conversations

Students engage in whole-class, small-group, and partner discussions during every lesson. The chart below provides prompt frames and response frames that will help students at different language proficiency levels interact with each other in meaningful ways.

You may wish to post these frames in the classroom for student reference.

CORE SKILL	PROMPT FRAMES	RESPONSE FRAMES
Elaborate and Ask Questions	Can you tell me more about it? Can you give me some details? Can you be more specific? What do you mean by...? How or why is it important?	I think it means that... In other words... It's important because... It's similar to when...
Support Ideas with Evidence	Can you give any examples from the text? What are some examples from other texts? What evidence do you see for that? How can you justify that idea? Can you show me where the text says that?	The text says that... An example from another text is... According to... Some evidence that supports that is...
Build On or Challenge Partner's Ideas	What do you think of the idea that...? Can we add to this idea? Do you agree? What are other ideas / points of view? What else do we need to think about? How does that connect to the idea...?	I would add that... I want to follow up on your idea... Another way to look at it is... What you said made me think of...
Paraphrase	What do we know so far? To recap, I think that... I'm not sure that was clear. How can we relate what I said to the topic / question?	So, you are saying that... Let me see if I understand you... Do you mean that...? In other words... It sounds like you are saying that...
Determine the Main Idea and Key Details	What have we discussed so far? How can we summarize what we have talked about? What can we agree upon? What are main points or ideas we can share? What relevant details support the main points or ideas? What key ideas can we take away?	We can say that... The main idea seems to be... As a result of this conversation, we think that we should... The evidence suggests that...

Strategies for Classroom Discussion

Providing multiple opportunities to speak in the classroom and welcoming all levels of participation will motivate English learners to take part in class discussions and build oral proficiency. These basic teaching strategies will encourage whole class and small group discussions for all language proficiency levels of English learners.

✔ WAIT TIME/DIFFERENT RESPONSE

- Be sure to give students enough time to answer the question. They may need more time to process their ideas.
- Let them know that they can respond in different ways depending on their levels of proficiency. Students can:
  - » Answer in their native language; then you can rephrase in English.
  - » Ask a more proficient EL speaker to repeat the answer in English.
  - » Answer with nonverbal cues.

✔ ELABORATE

- If students give a one-word answer or a nonverbal clue, elaborate on the answer to model fluent speaking and grammatical patterns.
- Provide more examples or repeat the answer using proper academic language.

✔ ELICIT

- Prompt students to give a more comprehensive response by asking additional questions or guiding them to get an answer, such as *can you tell me more?*
- This strategy is very effective when students are analyzing Primary Sources.

✔ ASKING ABOUT MEANING

- Repeating an answer offers an opportunity to clarify the meaning of a response.
- Repeating answer allows you to model the proper form for a response. You can model how to answer in full sentences and use academic language.
- When you repeat the answer, correct any grammar or pronunciation errors.

EMERGING
- What is _____?
- What does _____ mean?
- _____ is _____.
- _____ means _____.

EXPANDING
- Could you tell me what _____ means?
- _____ is similar to _____.
- _____ is another way of saying _____.

BRIDGING
- Could you give me a definition of _____?
- Can you point to the evidence from the text?
- What is the best answer? Why?

✓ TALK ABOUT LEVEL OF UNDERSTANDING

EMERGING
- I understand. / I got it.
- I don't understand this word / sentence.

EXPANDING
- Could you tell me what _____ means?
- _____ is another way of saying _____.

BRIDGING
- I think I understand most of it.
- I'm not sure I understand this completely.

✓ STATE YOUR OPINION

EMERGING
- I think _____.

EXPANDING
- In my opinion, _____.

BRIDGING
- My opinion is that _____.

✓ AGREEING WITH SOMEONE'S OPINION

EMERGING
- I agree with your opinion or point.

EXPANDING
- I agree that _____.

BRIDGING
- I have the same opinion as _____. I think that _____.

✓ DISAGREEING WITH SOMEONE'S OPINION

EMERGING
- I don't agree with your opinion or point.

EXPANDING
- I don't agree that _____.

BRIDGING
- I can see your point. However, I think that _____.

Grade 3 Overview

	CHAPTER 1	CHAPTER 2
	pages 2–27	pages 28–53
	Communities in California	American Indians of the Local Region
	EQ How does geography impact California communities?	**EQ** How have California Indians influenced the local region?
Lesson 1	Where is my community?	Who lived in early California?
Lesson 2	What are some features of each region in California?	How did the land affect California Indians?
Lesson 3	What are the features of a coastal community?	How did California Indians change the land?
Lesson 4	How did valley communities develop?	How did California Indians use natural resources?
Lesson 5	How do people live in a desert community?	What defines a California Indian community?
Lesson 6	What makes a mountain community unique?	How do California Indian communities work?
Lesson 7		

CHAPTER 3	CHAPTER 4	CHAPTER 5
pages 54–79	pages 80–109	pages 110–127
How and Why Communities Changed Over Time	American Citizens, Symbols, and Government	Economics of the Local Region
EQ How has life changed for people in my community over time?	**EQ** How do our government and its citizens work together?	**EQ** How do people in a community meet their needs?
Why do people move to a new region?	Why is the Constitution of the United States important?	How do businesses use resources?
How did settlers and California Indians interact?	How do the branches of government work together?	How have goods and services changed over time?
How do communities of the past compare to today?	Why do communities need governments?	How do businesses make money?
How have people changed the land?	What are some rules that we must follow?	How can people spend money wisely?
How did my community develop?	How has citizenship changed over time?	
What makes my community special?	How have heroes helped their communities?	
	How can citizens build strong communities?	

Chapter 1

Communities in California

 **How Does Geography Impact California Communities?**

Pages 2–5

SPANISH COGNATES

comunidad

conservar

elevación

industria

(recursos) naturales

precipitación

región

Inquiry Journal, pages 2–5

Introduce the Chapter

Access Prior Knowledge Read the Essential Question aloud to students. Check that they understand the meaning of the verb *impact*. Explain that it means "affects, changes, or influences in some way." Ask: *How would you describe the state of California?* Elicit answers such as: California is big; it is next to the Pacific Ocean; it has deserts and mountains; and it is mostly warm or hot. Write the word *geography* on the board. Ask: *What does* geography *mean?* Explain that *geography* means the study of the Earth's surface. Have students discuss the various aspects of geography, such as climate, population, physical features of the land, and use of the land.

Research Questions Have students brainstorm in pairs "just right" research questions (neither too general nor too specific). Use examples and sentence frames to help them form questions:

"How do the physical features and climate of California affect the use of the land?" is **too general** because _____.	it has too many answers
"What kind of plant grows in the desert region?" is **too specific** because _____.	it has only one easy answer
"How does the geography differ in the four regions of California?" is **just right** because _____.	it has more than one answer, but not too many answers

Inquiry Project Help students understand the project they will complete at the end of the chapter. Review any vocabulary that they don't understand, such as *regions*, *identify*, *label*, and *mark*.

Word Rater Remind students that they will learn the meaning of these important words as they read through the chapter. They will make notes each time they learn something new about the word's meaning. Point out the cognates to Spanish speakers. Help them rate the words according to whether they "Know it," "Heard it," or "Don't know it."

Why Do Communities Develop?

Ask questions about any unfamiliar vocabulary words. Explain that the word *rural* means the countryside. A rural area is usually devoted to agriculture, or farming. Read the following sentence aloud:

> Many things can affect how communities develop.

Circle the words *can affect*. Explain that in this sentence, the helping verb *can* means *might or may*. The verb *affect* means *influence* or *make something change*. The sentence is explaining how many things cause a change in communities.

Connect Through Literature

Explain that *Nature's Note-taker* is a biography. Tell students that a biography is the story of a person's life. The story is told by someone else. Most biographies are written about people to inspire us. A biography tells the most interesting facts about a person's life.

Explain that John Muir loved nature, and he wrote about it every day. Write the following sentence from the biography on the board and read it aloud:

> He painted word pictures of the untamed West for others who could not visit those places.

Explain that this means John Muir used descriptive language to express his ideas. Write the following phrase on the board and read it aloud:

> a magic wand in nature's hand

Say: *Muir thought the branches of a pine tree swaying in the wind looked like a magic wand in nature's hand.* (Gesture a swaying magic wand.) *He could have just written that the pine tree branches swayed in the wind.* Point out that instead, Muir chose to use a metaphor, a word or phrase that compares one thing to another thing. Explain that metaphors help us form pictures in our minds as we read. They make writing more interesting and engaging.

Explain some terms and phrases in the biography:

gliding softly = moving slowly and smoothly

roaring storm = a loud, powerful storm

pine needles = the thin green leaves on the branches of pine trees

silky murmur = a small, smooth sound

minty scent = the smell of mint

wildernerness = a natural area with no houses or roads

passion for nature = great love for nature

COLLABORATE
Have students work in pairs to complete the Leveled Support activities.

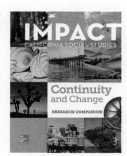
Pages 2–5

LEVELED SUPPORT

EMERGING Support students in expressing a fact with the sentence frame:
John Muir wrote about ____.

EXPANDING Encourage students to write at least one complete sentence with a fact.

BRIDGING Have students write several sentences about John Muir in their own words.

LESSON QUESTION

Where Is My Community?

CONTENT OBJECTIVES

- Explore more about your community.
- Examine different kinds of communities to understand why people choose to live in different places.
- Describe different kinds of communities, learn how to locate your community, and understand why people live in different places.

LANGUAGE OBJECTIVES

- Locate key details in the text.
- Recognize homophones *to*, *too* and *two*.
- Distinguish sentences from fragments.

Pages 6–11

Inquiry Journal, pages 6–11

Introduce the Lesson

Access Prior Knowledge Before presenting the Lesson Outcomes, read the Lesson Question and find out what students already know about their communities.

Say: *Our homes are next to other homes. Together these homes make neighborhoods. Neighborhoods form communities. Communities are larger than our neighborhoods. They have more people, shops, businesses, parks, and places to go. Our communities are part of our state*. Explain that our state is one of fifty states that make up our country, the United States of America.

COLLABORATE
Have students describe the things in their communities. Ask: *What are some shops, businesses, or parks in your community? What other kinds of places are in your community?*

Teach Content Vocabulary Write the following chart on the board to explain the meaning of important words in the text. For Spanish speakers, point out the cognuage.

SPANISH COGNATES

fértil

politico

Word	Part of Speech	Definition
California	noun	a state on the west coast of the United States
fertile	adjective	good for farming
county	noun	a large part of a state
political	adjective	relating to the government and how a place is governed

Say: *California has many farms. It is good for farming because the soil, or dirt, is very fertile. It is easy to grow things in California.* Ask: *What is the name of our county? What are some other counties in California?* Say: *You can look at a political map of California to see where the counties are located.*

COLLABORATE
Have students work in pairs to write sentences using each of the words.

Analyze the Source

Teach Academic Vocabulary Write the chart below on the board. Say each word aloud and have students repeat it. For Spanish speakers, point out the cognates.

Word	Part of Speech	Definition
contain	verb	have something inside
located	verb	be in a particular place
separate	verb	divide into parts
settle	verb	start living in a new place

Ask: *What are some things that our classroom <u>contains</u>? Where is our school <u>located</u>?* Elicit reasonable answers. Say: *County lines <u>separate</u> one county from another on a map.* Point out that *separate* can also be used as an adjective, meaning "different or not connected." Say: *Write your name on a <u>separate</u> piece of paper.* Ask: *What are some reasons that people <u>settled</u> in California?*

 COLLABORATE Have students work in pairs to do the Leveled Support activities.

Build Meaning Offer language support for the following phrases in the song lyrics:

greatest state of all = the best state

your dear mountains I adore = I love your mountains (poets and songwriters often use non-standard word order)

grand old ocean = huge ocean; the word "old" is used to show affection

her rugged shore = land along the ocean that is not smooth; songwriters and poets often use the female pronoun to refer to bodies of water.

California Counties

Unpack the Text Write the following sentence on the board and read it aloud:

They are imaginary lines drawn on maps to show how places are separated.

Point to the word *They*. Ask: *What does this word refer to?* (borders) Explain that the sentence tells you two things about borders. Underline *are imaginary lines drawn on maps*. Say: *First of all, borders are imaginary lines drawn on maps.* Then underline *show how places are separated*. Say: *Borders show how places are separated.* Finally, circle the word *to*. Say: *The word* to *connects these two pieces of information.*

ACADEMIC VOCABULARY

contain

located

separate

settle

SPANISH COGNATES

contener

separar

LEVELED SUPPORT

EMERGING The text contains three uses of the word "separate(d)." Help students identify the part of speech in each instance.

EXPANDING Have students locate each vocabulary word in context, then rewrite the sentence using a synonym (word or phrase) for the target vocabulary word.

BRIDGING Have students choose one academic vocabulary word and try to use it in the context of a different content area. For example, in math, you can "separate" one whole into four equal parts.

Pages 6–13

ACADEMIC VOCABULARY

offer

represent

actual

distance

SPANISH COGNATES

ofrecer

representar

distancia

LEVELED SUPPORT

EMERGING Provide students with sentence frames for speaking practice during the game. *There are many homes, businesses, and apartments in an urban area.*

EXPANDING Have students give an example for each game item. *In an urban area, you will find parks, museums, and many shops. For example, there are many shops in San Francisco.*

BRIDGING Have students lead the game. Challenge them to use complete sentences to describe a community.

Research Companion, pages 6–13

Teach Academic Vocabulary Write the chart below on the board. Say each word aloud and have students repeat it. For Spanish speakers, point out the cognates.

Word	Part of Speech	Definition
offer	verb	provide something
represent	verb	be a symbol of something
actual	adjective	real
distance	noun	the amount of space between two places

Ask: *Many cites and towns offer ways to have fun. What does your community offer? What does a scale on a map represent? What do you think is the distance between our city/town and New York City?* Write students' guesses on the board. Find out the real distance. Say: *The actual distance is [# of miles].*

Vocabulary Word Game: Urban, Rural, Suburban

Materials: Three index cards for each student, a list of descriptions of communities
Directions: Refer to the Leveled Support as you facilitate the game. Have students write the following words, *urban, rural, suburban*, one on each card. Ask students to guess whether a community is urban, rural, or suburban. Describe a type of community and have students hold up the appropriate card.

For example, *large population, many businesses, lots of traffic*. Then invite volunteers to create sentences based on your clues.

Communities in California

Unpack the Text Write the following sentence on the board and read it aloud:

> Many people who live in the suburban areas travel into urban areas for work.

Explain that this sentence is about a group of people and what they do. Underline *Many people who live in suburban areas*. Point out the word *who* is used to connect *Many people* with information about those people, specifically that they *live in suburban areas*. Say: *When you want to give additional information about a person or a group of people, use the word* who *to connect ideas*. Point to the phrase you underlined. Ask: *What do many people who live in the suburb areas do?* Elicit the second part of the sentence, *travel into urban areas for work*. For additional simplification, substitute the entire subject with a pronoun, rewriting the sentence as follows:

> They travel into urban areas for work.

Build Meaning Offer language support for the following phrases:

map key = list of symbols and what they mean

compass rose = shows where north, south, east, and west are on a map

intermediate direction = directions in between north, south, east, and west

stand for = are symbols of, mean the same thing as

Homophones *to, too, and two* Distribute copies of the graphic organizer to students. Review the homophones *to*, *too*, and *two*. Say: *I am going to the store. The word* to *means "in the direction of" or "toward." I am going to the library,* too. *In this sentence* too *means "also." I am also going to the library. I need two books. Two* is the number of books.

COLLABORATE Have students work in pairs to use each meaning in a sentence.

To (Preposition)	Too (Adverb)	Two (noun/adjective)
in the direction of; toward	also; in addition	cardinal number (one, two) / amount

Inquiry Journal, pages 12–13

Report Your Findings

Demonstrate Understanding Review the **Report Your Findings** task with the students.

Think About It Explain to students that they will write a paragraph about the type of community they want to live in. Remind them of the meaning of *urban*, *suburban*, and *rural*. Have students use the following sentence frames to make notes about their opinions.

EMERGING   I think _____.

EXPANDING   In my opinion, _____.

BRIDGING   My opinion is that _____.

Write About It During the writing task, monitor and offer support with vocabulary, sentence formation, spelling, and mechanics.

Talk About It Tell students they will explain or give examples from the text to another classmate. Have them use the following sentence frames to give examples for their opinions.

EMERGING   I think _____ because _____.

EXPANDING   For example, _____.

BRIDGING   According to the text, _____.

COLLABORATE Foster interaction by having students of different proficiencies work together as they relate their information to the Lesson Question.

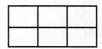

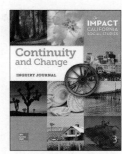
Pages 12–13

What Are Some Features of Each Region in California?

CONTENT OBJECTIVES

- Explore the features of California's geographic regions.
- Examine how communities in California developed and how people live today.
- Identify California's geographic regions and give details about each of them.

LANGUAGE OBJECTIVES

- Locate key details in the text.
- Recognize main idea and details.
- Find and use prepositional phrases in the text.

Pages 14–19

Inquiry Journal, pages 14–19

Introduce the Lesson

Access Prior Knowledge Before presenting the Lesson Outcomes, read the Lesson Question and find out what students already know about the features of each region in California. Students have already learned some things about California. They may recall that it is a large state. There are suburban, urban, and rural communities. Some communities have larger populations than others. The land, water, and climate are different throughout California's communities. Say: *In this lesson you will learn much more about the state of California.*

COLLABORATE Have students work in pairs to describe the features of their community. Have them describe the climate and name any landforms they know.

Teach Content Vocabulary Write the following chart on the board. Say each word aloud and have students repeat it. For Spanish speakers, point out the cognates.

SPANISH COGNATES

valle

geografía

sitio histórico

Word	Part of Speech	Definition
valley	noun	an area of low land between hills or mountains
geography	noun	the study of the surface of the Earth
historic site	noun	a place that is important in history
landmark	noun	an important building or place

Explain that these words are used to describe the features of a region. Say: *The geography, or the study of the landforms in California, is very interesting. There are mountains and the land between mountains called valleys. Some landforms are historic sites, such as Yosemite Park. Yosemite Park is a landmark.*

PRODUCTIVE Have students name a landmark or historic site and describe its geography in their own words.

Analyze the Source

Teach Academic Vocabulary Write the chart below on the board. Say each word aloud and have students repeat it. For Spanish speakers, point out the cognates.

Word	Part of Speech	Definition
natural	adjective	plants or objects not made by people
create	verb	make
national	adjective	relating to a particular country
protect	verb	keep someone or something safe

Ask: *Have you <u>created</u> anything recently? What did you create? What are some <u>natural</u> things near where you live? What are some <u>national</u> parks in California? What are some things you can do to help <u>protect</u> our environment?*

COLLABORATE Have students work in pairs to make sentences using the words.

Parks in California

Unpack the Text Write the following sentence on the board and read it aloud:

> Point Reyes National Seashore brings many visitors to California's coast each year.

Explain that the sentence is easier to understand if we split it into two parts. First, use the word *visitors* as the subject of the sentence. Ask: *Who comes to the California coast each year?* Say: *Visitors come to the California Coast each year.* Then ask: *Why do visitors come to the California coast? What is one thing they want to see?* Elicit that visitors want to see the Point Reyes National Seashore. Explain that in this case, the word *brings* means "makes people want to go somewhere."

Build Meaning Offer language support for the following phrases:

national park = a large park owned and operated by the government for the use by the people

John Muir = a man who worked to create laws to protect California's natural land

miners and settlers = people who mine and settle; adding *-er* to the end of a verb changes it into a noun that describes the person who does the action

he founded the Sierra Club = he started the Sierra Club

SPANISH COGNATES

natural

crear

nacional

proteger

LEVELED SUPPORT

EMERGING Practice the sentence structure using community-based role-plays that reinforce vocabulary. For example, pretend to be a supermarket worker and ask: *What brings you to the super market today? (I need food.)*

EXPANDING/ BRIDGING Ask students to frame the sentence as a cause-effect relationship (cause: People want to see Point Reyes National Seashore; effect: People visit the coast). Challenge them to use similar language to describe other cause-and-effect relationships in the text.

Pages 14–23

ACADEMIC VOCABULARY

feature

affect

surround

adapt

SPANISH COGNATES

afectar

adaptar

Research Companion, pages 14–23

Teach Academic Vocabulary Write the chart below on the board. Say each word aloud and have students repeat it. For Spanish speakers, point out the cognates.

Word	Part of Speech	Definition
feature	noun	an important part or quality of something
affect	verb	cause something to change
surround	verb	be all around something or someone
adapt	verb	change something to work better in a different situation

Have students find the words in the text (pages 14 and 17). Challenge them to paraphrase each sentence to demonstrate their understanding. For example, "It is <u>surrounded</u> by mountains" could become "It has mountains all around it." Challenge them to use each word in a new sentence about themselves, California, or another content area.

Vocabulary Word Game: California Bingo

Materials: Blank bingo card with the game title on it, terms on cards
Directions: Make a list of some of the names and terms in the lesson. Give each student a blank bingo card with the game title on it. (Teacher Tip: Have more terms than boxes on cards.) Have students fill in one term or name in random order in each empty box. Write definitions or descriptions of each name or term on small cards. Play Bingo: The caller reads the definition and students cover it on the card if they find the term.

California's Regions

Unpack the Text Write the following sentence from "The Coast" on the board:

> People can fish, watch sea lions and seals at the harbor, or take boats out on the water.

Say: *This sentence explains many reasons why people like the California coast. Let's deconstruct this sentence and make it easier to understand.* Underline the phrase *People can.* Remind students that *can* is used before a verb to tell about ability. Invite students to name the three verbs in the sentence. Ask: *What can people do?* Circle each one: *fish, watch, take.* Write three new sentences:

> People can fish.

> People can watch sea lions and seals at the harbor.

> People can take boats out on the water.

PRODUCTIVE Have students create sentences about your town using the same structure. For example, *In our town, people can ski, visit City Park and City Museum, and eat fresh fruit from the farms.*

Build Meaning Provide language support for the following phrases:

sea level = the level of the surface of the ocean

mountain runoff = the flow of water from snow melting on mountains

unlimited supply = an amount that will never run out

dams, canals, and pipelines = human-made structures that control and direct water flow

Prepositions and Prepositional Phrases Remind students that prepositions are often short words that show the relationship between a noun and other words in the text. Write some common prepositions on the board:

of	to	in	at	from
into	with	for	on	by

Review prepositional phrases. Write the following prepositional phrases on the board. Read each phrase and underline the preposition.

<u>to</u> the east   <u>into</u> the Sacramento River

<u>in</u> ships   <u>on</u> the water

Inquiry Journal, pages 20–21

Report Your Findings

Demonstrate Understanding Review the **Report Your Findings** task with students.

Think About It Review key vocabulary words. Assist students in listing and describing each of California's geographic regions. Explain that they will be asked to choose which of California's geographic regions they think is the most interesting.

Write About It Place students in groups of three or four. Remind them of the Lesson Question: *What Are Some Features of Each Region in California?* Remind students that when stating an opinion there is no right or wrong answer. However, opinions must be supported by facts.

Talk About It Have students state their opinion using the following sentence frames:

EMERGING   I think the most interesting region in California is
_____. because it is _____,
_____, and _____.

EXPANDING/BRIDGING   In my opinion, _____ is the most
interesting because _____. In addition,
_____. I also think _____.

Provide assistance with vocabulary, pronunciation, and idea formation as needed. During the writing task, monitor and offer support with vocabulary, sentence formation, spelling, and mechanics.

COLLABORATE Foster interaction by having students of different proficiencies discuss their opinions and the supporting reasons as they answer the Essential Question.

LEVELED SUPPORT

EMERGING Have students work in pairs to skim the text to find other examples of prepositional phrases.

EXPANDING/ BRIDGING Have students write their own prepositional phrases, using some of the most common prepositions.

Pages 20–21

What Are the Features of a Coastal Community?

CONTENT OBJECTIVES

- Explore the coastal region of California.
- Examine the geography of the coastal region and how it affects the people who live there.
- Identify the features of California's coastal communities and how they affect the community.

LANGUAGE OBJECTIVES

- Locate key details in the text.
- Recognize sentences and fragments.
- Understand that *where* in a sentence indicates a place.

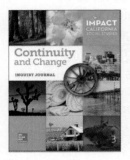

Pages 22–27

Inquiry Journal, pages 22–27

Introduce the Lesson

Access Prior Knowledge Before presenting the Lesson Outcomes, read the Lesson Question and find out what students already know about features of a coastal community. Discuss the words *features, coastal,* and *community* as needed. Encourage students to think about things they do near the ocean, and things they might use that come from the ocean. Say: *You have been studying the state of California. California has many different kinds of regions. It has hot deserts, valleys of fertile soil, high mountains, the world's tallest trees, and many national parks. In this lesson you will learn about the coastal areas and the variety of plant and animal life in California.*

COLLABORATE Have students work in pairs to name cities near the coast of California. What do they know about these cities?

Teach Content Vocabulary Write the following chart on the board. Say each word aloud and have students repeat it. For Spanish speakers, point out the cognate.

SPANISH COGNATE

costera

Word	Part of Speech	Definition
cliff	noun	high, steep rocks, often next to the ocean
tide pool	noun	a small area of ocean water that is left on the beach when the tide goes out
debris	noun	trash; garbage
coastal	adjective	describes a region next to an ocean or large lake

Say: *California is a <u>coastal</u> state. What does that mean? Can you think of some other coastal states?* Explain what *tide* means. Ask: *Is the water in a <u>tide pool</u> usually warmer or colder than the water in the ocean? Why? Is it safe to walk near the edge of a <u>cliff</u>? Why or why not? Have you ever seen <u>debris</u> on the beach? How do you think it gets there?*

COLLABORATE Have students work in pairs to make sentences using each of the words.

Analyze the Source

Teach Academic Vocabulary Write the chart below on the board. Say each word aloud and have students repeat it. For Spanish speakers, point out the cognates.

Word	Part of Speech	Definition
explore	verb	think about something very carefully
research	noun	a detailed study of a topic in order to discover new information
summary	noun	a short description that gives the main facts or ideas about something
investigate	verb	discover all the facts about something

Say: *When we explore a topic, we think and talk about it. What topic are we exploring in this unit? When we research or investigate a topic, we try to find new information about it. What resources can we use to research a topic?*

COLLABORATE Have students work in pairs to write sentences using each of the words.

Sentences and Fragments Distribute copies of the graphic organizer to students and have them do the Leveled Support activities. Remind them that a sentence is a complete thought. A sentence contains a subject and a verb. Read the groups of words in the first column, and have students write whether each is a sentence or a fragment in the second column.

	Sentence or Fragment?
California's coast is hundreds of miles long.	
California's coastal communities.	
Rocky land and mild climate.	
California is known for sandy beaches.	

Build Meaning Offer language support for the the following phrases:

all the way through = from beginning to end

restate the topic = tell about the idea in a different way

ACADEMIC VOCABULARY

explore

research

summary

investigate

SPANISH COGNATES

explorar

investigar

GRAPHIC ORGANIZER

LEVELED SUPPORT

EMERGING Give students a mini-lesson on the parts of a sentence: subject and predicate.

EXPANDING Have students change the fragments into complete sentences.

BRIDGING Have students create their own exercises. Tell them to write two fragments and two sentences and trade with a partner. Partners identify each other's fragments and sentences.

Pages 24–31

ACADEMIC VOCABULARY

transport

erosion

goods

rely

SPANISH COGNATES

transporte

erosión

LEVELED SUPPORT

EMERGING Write each academic word on one index card, and its definition on another. Have students work together to match the word with the correct definition.

EXPANDING/BRIDGING Have students work in pairs to write a question and an answer for each of the words.

Research Companion, pages 24–31

Teach Academic Vocabulary Write the chart below on the board. Say each word aloud and have students repeat it. For Spanish speakers, point out the cognates.

Word	Part of Speech	Definition
transport	verb	move people or goods from one place to another
erosion	noun	the way the surface of the Earth is worn away by weather, water, or other causes
goods	noun	items that are made to be sold
rely	verb	depend on

Point out that _transport_ can also be used as a noun, meaning vehicles such as cars, buses, trains, and ships. Ask: _How might_ <u>erosion</u> _hurt a coastline community? What_ <u>goods</u> _do you use that come from a coastal community? What are some ways to_ <u>transport</u> _goods from one place to another? Which way do you think is fastest? What do people in coastal communities_ <u>rely</u> _on?_

 INTERPRETIVE Have students work in pairs to complete the Leveled Support activities.

Build Meaning Offer language support for the following phrases:

obligation to the people = something that you must do for the benefit of the citizens in an area

optimize our capabilities and our resources = use our abilities (capabilities) and the tools we have (resources) to make something as good as possible (optimize)

Making a Living Along the Coast

Unpack the Text Write the following sentence on the board and read it aloud:

A dock is a flat surface where boats or ships are tied up to be loaded and unloaded.

Explain that this sentence tells you three things about a dock. Elicit: (1) _A dock is a flat surface._ (2) _Boats and ships are tied up to a dock._ (3) _Boats and ships are loaded and unloaded at a dock._ Now draw attention to the words and phrases that connect these ideas. Circle the word _where_. Say: _A dock is a flat surface_ <u>where</u> _boats and ships are tied up._ Circle the phrase _to be_. Say: _This explains why. Why are boats tied up to a dock?_ <u>To be</u> _loaded and unloaded._

Vocabulary Word Game: Concentration

Materials: Index cards containing vocabulary words and definitions (one vocabulary word or definition per card)

Directions: Play concentration. Match the vocabulary words with the definitions. Place the cards face down in rows. Have students look for pairs. Ask a student to draw a card. Have the student read the word and then select another card. If the cards match, keep the cards face up. If not, turn both cards face down.

Inquiry Journal, pages 28–29

Report Your Findings

Demonstrate Understanding Review the **Report Your Findings** task with the students.

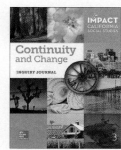

Pages 28–29

Think About It Ask students to picture a California coastal community in their minds. Have them recall information they have gathered from the text. Ask for volunteers to describe some of the features they remember. List these features on the board. Remind students to use vocabulary words in their descriptions. Have students turn to a partner and take turns describing a coastal community.

EMERGING Have students work together answer the Lesson Question by completing sentence frames.

The southern coast has sandy _____ and warm _____.

The coast is home to many different kinds of _____ and _____.

Many people work in the _____ and shipping industries.

EXPANDING Have students work in a group to list the key details: fishing and shipping, ports, beaches, and nature. Help them explain the features of California's coastal communities by making a sentence for each detail.

BRIDGING Have students work in pairs to write several sentences describing California's coastal communities. Tell them to include some of the following: beaches, industry, and nature.

Write About It Place students in small groups of three or four. Remind them of the Lesson Question: *What Are the Features of a Coastal Community?* Have students choose one of the types of coastal communities they have read about. Instruct them to write a paragraph describing the features of that community. Remind them to include the physical features, resources, industries and recreational activities found in the coastal community,

Provide assistance with vocabulary, pronunciation, and idea formation as needed. During the writing task, monitor and offer support with vocabulary, sentence formation, spelling, and mechanics.

COLLABORATE
Foster interaction by having students of different proficiencies discuss their ideas as they answer the Lesson Question.

How Did Valley Communities Develop?

CONTENT OBJECTIVES

- Explore the valley region of California.
- Examine how the geography of California's valleys affects the people who live there.
- Identify the valley regions and describe how the communities were affected by the land.

LANGUAGE OBJECTIVES

- Understand and locate key details in the text.
- Recognize sentence fragments.
- Answer questions about the text.

pages 30–35

SPANISH COGNATE

conservar

LEVELED SUPPORT

EMERGING Create some cloze sentences to practice the vocabulary. For example, *The farmers gathered grapes from the <u>field</u>. The <u>crop</u> was successful.*

EXPANDING Have students list examples for each word, for example, things that you can <u>conserve</u>, or different <u>crops</u>.

BRIDGING Have students create idea webs. For each word, they create a web with related words, examples, sample sentences, and even drawings.

Inquiry Journal, pages 30–35

Introduce the Lesson

Access Prior Knowledge Before presenting the Lesson Outcomes, read the Lesson Question and find out what students already know about how valley communities developed. If needed, explain that valleys are flat lands in between mountains and hills.

PRODUCTIVE Preview the pictures in the Inquiry Journal. Ask students to predict what they will read in the text: *What is the climate? What is the soil like? What kinds of industries are there in valleys?*

Teach Content Vocabulary Write the following chart on the board. Say each word aloud and have students repeat it. For Spanish speakers, point out the cognate.

Word	Part of Speech	Definition
field	noun	a flat area of land where food is grown
crop	noun	a plant that is grown by farmers
settlement	noun	a place where people make a home after coming from somewhere else
conserve	verb	save or protect

Explain that *conserve* and *settle* are base words. Create a chart showing some related words:

Verbs	Nouns
conserve	conservation conservationist
settle	settler settlement

PRODUCTIVE Have students make sentences using the content vocabulary and the verbs and nouns in the chart.

Analyze the Source

Teach Academic Vocabulary Write the chart below on the board. Say each word aloud and have students repeat it. For Spanish speakers, point out the cognates.

Word	Part of Speech	Definition
signal	noun	something that shows something is likely to happen
form	verb	start to exist
related	adjective	connected; having to do with one another
develop	verb	grow and change

Ask questions to check understanding: *What is a signal that a traffic light is going to turn red?* (It turns yellow.) Ask: *How are rain and crops related?* (Crops need rain to grow.) Ask: *How do you think clouds form? How do friendships sometimes develop? That is, how do you become friends with someone?*

 COLLABORATE Have students work in pairs to make sentences with the words.

How Did Valley Communities Develop?

Unpack the Text Write the following sentence on the board, and read it aloud:

> Valleys have rich soil and a mild climate that are good for growing crops.

Explain that this sentence is part of a caption—the words that describe a photograph and provide more details. Point out that this sentence has two clauses. Underline *Valleys have rich soil and a mild climate* and *are good for growing crops*. Circle the word *that*. Explain that the word *that* condenses, or joins, clauses in a sentence. The word *that*, in this sentence, refers back to the *rich soil and a mild climate*. We could write this sentence as two sentences:

> Valleys have rich soil and a mild climate.
> Rich soil and a mild climate are good for growing crops.

Cross out *Rich soil and a mild climate* in the second sentence and replace it with *that*. Say: *We can use the word that to connect the sentences and make one sentence.*

Build Meaning Offer language support for terms and phrases in the instructions:

based on the photo = by looking at the photo

affect vs. effect = "affect" is a verb that means change or influence; "effect" is usually used as a noun that means the result or change that was caused by something. "Effect" can also be used as a verb that means to cause.

examine = look at carefully

clues = pieces of information that help you find answers

Pages 32–39

ACADEMIC VOCABULARY

provide

ideal

produce

machine

SPANISH COGNATES

proveer

ideal

producir

máquina

Research Companion, pages 32–39

Teach Academic Vocabulary Write the chart below on the board. Say each word aloud and have students repeat it. For Spanish speakers, point out the cognates.

Word	Part of Speech	Definition
provide	verb	supply with something
ideal	adjective	perfect, well-suited
produce	verb	make or create
machine	noun	a piece of equipment with moving parts that uses power to do a particular job

Ask: *What do farms underline(provide)? What kinds of fruits does California underline(produce)? What are some underline(machines) that you use every day? Some people say that California has an underline(ideal) climate, or weather. Do you agree?*

COLLABORATE Have students work in pairs to make their own sentences about California using the academic vocabulary. Challenge them to think back to information they learned in previous chapters.

Settling in the Valleys

Unpack the Text Write the following sentence on the board and read it aloud:

> Their way of life was shaped by the natural resources around them.

Underline the words *was shaped by*. Say: *This sentence uses the past passive form of the verb* shape. *We can rearrange the words in the sentence to use an active verb form instead.* Circle *the natural resources around them*. Then write the same words below the original sentence. Underline the word *shaped* and write it in the new sentence. Finally, circle *Their way of life* and write it in the new sentence. Cross out *was* and *by*.

Read the new sentence: *The natural resources around them shaped their way of life*.

Build Meaning Offer language support for the following phrases:

farming remains important = farming is still important today

raising livestock = keeping animals on a farm

was formed in = "was formed" is the passive verb form; the phrase can be rephrased in an active voice as "Some people formed the Central Valley Project in 1935 ..."

water transport system = a group of things that are connected to move water

Sentences Review the definition of a sentence with the students. Remind them that a sentence is a complete thought and that it contains a subject and a verb. Write the following sets of words on the board. Distribute the graphic organizer, and have students write the sentences and fragments in the correct column.

The state capital, Sacramento

Trees that grew in the area

Rivers and streams provided fish.

more money and better working conditions

Almonds are a popular and healthy food.

Sentence	Fragment

COLLABORATE
Have students work in pairs to complete the Leveled Support activities.

Inquiry Journal, pages 36–37

Report Your Findings

Demonstrate Understanding Review the **Report Your Findings** task with the students.

Think About It Review key vocabulary words. Assist students in describing how valley communities were formed. Help them explain how valley communities changed over time. Tell students they will be asked to use facts from the text to explain how valleys were formed and how they changed over time.

Write About It Place students in small groups of three or four. Remind them of the Lesson Question: *How Did Valley Communities Develop?* Remind students to use facts from the text to explain what caused the valley communities to form and how they changed over time.

EMERGING   I think _____ because _____.

EXPANDING   The text shows _____.

BRIDGING   Evidence from the text indicates that _____.

Provide assistance with vocabulary, pronunciation, and idea formation as needed. During the writing task, monitor and offer support with vocabulary, sentence formation, spelling, and mechanics.

COLLABORATE
Foster interaction by having students of different proficiencies discuss their paragraphs as they answer the Essential Question.

Connect to the Essential Question Remind students of the meaning of *geography*.

GRAPHIC ORGANIZER

LEVELED SUPPORT

EMERGING Have students identify the nouns and verbs in the sentences.

EXPANDING/ BRIDGING Ask students to explain why the fragments aren't sentences. Have them rewrite the fragments to make them sentences.

Pages 36–37

How Do People Live in a Desert Community?

CONTENT OBJECTIVES

- Explore the desert region of California and explore how the land affects the people that live there.
- Examine how a region's environment will help you learn more about how geography impacts California's communities.
- Describe what a desert is and what life is like for people who live there.

LANGUAGE OBJECTIVES

- Locate key details in the text.
- Review cause-and-effect sentences with *because*.
- Understand compound words.
- Answer questions in the text.
- Understand the possessive pronoun *its*.

Pages 38–43

Inquiry Journal, pages 38–43

Introduce the Lesson

Access Prior Knowledge Before presenting the Lesson Outcomes, read the Lesson Question and find out what students already know about deserts. Invite them to also share any experiences they have visiting, watching movies, or reading about deserts. For example, they may think deserts are hot and dry with few plants. Some students may have visited one of California's desert regions. Say: *In studying the state of California, we have learned about the coastal communities and the towns of the Central Valley. We have learned that the geography and climate is very important for a community. How might the geography and climate in a desert affect the people, plants, and animals who live in a desert community?*

PRODUCTIVE Have students work in pairs to share what they know about deserts, and then report their partner's ideas to the class. Elicit language as needed. For example, *My partner is Gina. Gina visited Death Valley National Park. (Did Gina think it was hot or cold?) It was hot. And there wasn't any water.*

Teach Content Vocabulary Write the following chart on the board. Say each word aloud and have students repeat it. For Spanish speakers, point out the cognate.

Word	Part of Speech	Definition
root	noun	the part of a plant that grows underground
harsh	adjective	difficult, dangerous, and unpleasant
North Pole	noun	the place on Earth's surface that is farthest north
temperature	noun	how hot or cold something is

Ask questions to check understanding: *Why do you think plants have <u>roots</u>?* Say: *The <u>North Pole</u> has a <u>harsh</u> climate. It has very low <u>temperatures</u>. Can you think of another place with a harsh climate?*

COLLABORATE Have students work in pairs to do the Leveled Support activities.

SPANISH COGNATE

temperatura

LEVELED SUPPORT

EMERGING Use cloze sentences to check for understanding.

EXPANDING/BRIDGING Give a scenario and have students decide which vocabulary word best fits your description.

Analyze the Source

Teach Academic Vocabulary Write the chart below on the board. Say each word aloud and have students repeat it. For Spanish speakers, point out the cognates.

Word	Part of Speech	Definition
impact	verb	affect
element	noun	part of something
limited	adjective	not very great in amount or number
judgment	noun	opinion about something, usually related to whether it is good or bad

ACADEMIC VOCABULARY

impact

element

limited

judgment

SPANISH COGNATES

impacto

elemento

limitado

COLLABORATE Have students review previous lessons and use academic vocabulary words to talk about the other regions in California.

Build Meaning Offer language support for the following phrases:

long period of time = a large block of time, usually many years

little relief from the heat = The heat is very unpleasant and there are few ways to get help or feel better.

as well = also

life-or-death situation = when something is very dangerous

Climate Helps Describe a Region

Unpack the Text Write the following sentence on the board and read it aloud:

Its limited precipitation means there is little relief from the heat.

Say: *This is a long sentence with some hard words. Let's look at each part of the sentence closely.* First, review possessive pronouns with students. Point out that *Its* replaces the word *region* in the previous sentence. Say: *This sentence tells us about the region's limited precipitation.* Point out that we don't use an apostrophe with *its*. *It's* always means *it is*.

Now review the vocabulary with students. Explain that *limited* means a small amount or not very much. *Precipitation* means rain or snow. Say: *We are reading about California's desert. We know there's no snow in the desert, so* precipitation *must mean* rain *in this sentence*. Explain that *limited precipitation* is a scientific (or academic) way of saying *very little rain*. Underline <u>little relief</u>. Explain that *relief* means an end to pain or discomfort. For example, when a toothache goes away, we feel relief. When we swim in cool water on a hot day, we feel relief. The sentence is telling us there is little, or not much, relief from the heat in California's desert. Why? Underline the word <u>means</u>. Explain that *means* in a sentence can show a cause-and-effect relationship. Draw an arrow from *limited precipitation* to *little relief from the heat*. There is little relief <u>because</u> there is limited precipitation.

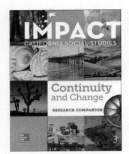

Pages 40–47

ACADEMIC VOCABULARY

unique

valuable

establish

survive

SPANISH COGNATES

único

valioso

establecer

Research Companion, pages 40–47

Teach Academic Vocabulary Write the chart below on the board. Say each word aloud and have students repeat it. For Spanish speakers, point out the cognates.

Word	Part of Speech	Definition
unique	adjective	special and different; one-of-a-kind
valuable	adjective	worth a lot of money; very helpful and important
establish	verb	start a business, organization, or community that lasts a long time
survive	verb	continue to exist while in a difficult situation

After discussing the definitions above, connect these academic words to other ideas students have discussed in Chapter 1. Say: *What is unique about our town? What valuable metal brought many people to California in the 1800s? Why were many towns established along the coast in California? What do crops need to survive?*

 PRODUCTIVE Have students work in pairs to make sentences with the words.

Build Meaning Offer language support for the following phrases:

limited vegetation = not a lot of plants

lack of water = not enough water

contribute to = be a factor in, help to cause

make a living = earn money to pay for things you need

on the other hand = used to compare two different things or situations

Exploring a Desert Environment

Unpack the Text Write the following sentences on the board and read it aloud:

> The desert can be a tough place to live. But it has become easier because people now bring water there.

Review cause-and-effect sentences with students. Ask: *Do you see a word here that tells about a cause and an effect?* Circle *because*. Say: *Remember, when we see the word* because *in a sentence, we know that something has happened as a result of something else.* Reread the first sentence. Say: *The first sentence tells us that the desert can be a tough, or hard, place to live. Why?* Elicit that deserts are hot and dry. Ask: *But living in the desert is easier now. Why?* Elicit that people can bring water to the desert now. Write the following on the board:

Cause: People bring water.

Effect: Living in the desert became easier.

Point out that the conjunction *because* joins the two phrases. One clause is the cause (people bring water) and the other clause is the effect (living became easier).

 INTERPRETIVE Have pairs of students look for other cause-and-effect sentences in the text. Have them identify the cause and the effect.

Compound Words Remind students that compound words are two words joined together to make a new word. Sometimes a hyphen is used. Say: *Looking at the two words that make a compound word helps you understand the new meaning.* Write the following words on the board:

Southeast   rainfall   surefooted   bighorn   black-tailed

wildflowers   underground   red-spotted   overnight sometimes

Distribute copies of the graphic organizer to students, with the example of *rainfall* included. Have them do the Leveled Support activities.

Compound Word	Word +	Word	Definition
rainfall	rain	fall	the amount of rain that falls

Inquiry Journal, pages 44–45

Report Your Findings

Demonstrate Understanding Review the **Report Your Findings** task with the students.

Think About It Review key vocabulary words. Assist students in describing the characteristics of a desert environment. Have them skim the text for information to get the discussion started. Help them explain how the environment affects a desert community.

 INTERPRETIVE As a warm-up to the writing activity, have students compare and contrast the desert regions and valley regions. Encourage them to consider geography, climate, and community.

Write About It Place students in pairs. Remind them of the Lesson Question: *How do people live in a desert community?* Have students write a paragraph explaining how the environment affects a desert community. Remind students to begin their paragraphs with an opening statement. Ask students to explain how the geography, extreme temperatures, and lack of water affect the way the people and animals live.

Provide assistance with vocabulary, pronunciation, and idea formation as needed. During the writing task, monitor and offer support with vocabulary, sentence formation, spelling, and mechanics.

GRAPHIC ORGANIZER

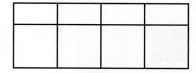

Pages 44–45

LEVELED SUPPORT

EMERGING Have students complete the second and third columns of the chart.

EXPANDING Have students write the definitions of the words they know in the last column of the chart.

BRIDGING Have students choose three words and use them in a sentence.

LESSON QUESTION

What Makes a Mountain Community Unique?

CONTENT OBJECTIVES

- Explore how the land affects California's mountain communities.
- Examine how the geography of a region will help us learn how the land affects the community.
- Describe California's mountain region.

LANGUAGE OBJECTIVES

- Understand sentence structure.
- Understand proper nouns and common nouns.
- Understand and use the transition word *however*.

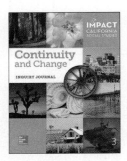

pages 46–51

SPANISH COGNATE

minería

Inquiry Journal, pages 46–51

Introduce the Lesson

Access Prior Knowledge Before presenting the Lesson Outcomes, read the Lesson Question and find out what students already know about a mountain region. Using landform maps, ask students to describe the geography of a mountain region. Ask: *Has anyone lived in a mountain region or visited a mountain? What did you see there? What kinds of plants and animals live there? What is interesting in the mountains? What is unusual, or unique? What do you think makes a mountain region different from other regions?*

COLLABORATE Explain to students how geography of a region affects the way people live. Have students work in pairs to discuss the geography of a mountain community in California.

Teach Content Vocabulary Write the chart below on the board. For Spanish speakers, point out the cognate.

Word	Part of Speech	Definition
landscape	noun	an area in the countryside
peak	noun	the highest point of a mountain
mining	noun	the work of getting gold, coal, and other things out of the ground
settler	noun	someone who moves to a new place to live

Explain that some <u>settlers</u> came to the mountain regions for <u>mining</u>. Say: *Mining is a job in which people dig in the ground looking for minerals. They look for precious metals, such as gold and silver.* Point out that *mining* can also be used as an adjective, as in *mining town*, and a verb, for example: *The men mined for gold.* Ask: *What is the top of a mountain called?* (a <u>peak</u>) *What is the region around the mountain called?* (a <u>landscape</u>)

COLLABORATE Have students work in pairs to write sentences using two of the words. Then have them read each other's sentences aloud.

Analyze the Source

Teach Academic Vocabulary Write the chart below on the board. Say each word aloud and have students repeat it. For Spanish speakers, point out the cognates.

Word	Part of Speech	Definition
eventually	adverb	at the end of a period of time
decline	verb	become less or not as great
skilled	adjective	good at doing something
discover	noun	find or learn something for the first time

Remind students that some words can be used as different parts of speech. For example, _decline_ can also be used as a noun. It means the amount that something becomes less. Say: _The number of settlers moving to the mountain region was in decline._ Ask questions to check understanding of the information. Call on volunteers to use the words in their own sentences.

What Makes a Region Appealing?

Unpack the Text Write the following sentences on the board:

> A few people hope to find gold. Most people, however, come for other reasons.

Read both sentences aloud. Explain that the second sentence contains a transition word. Say: _This sentence shows a contrast. We know there is a contrast when we see the word_ however. _This means you should look for a comparison. Sometimes, as in this sentence, only one thing is mentioned. You have to look at the sentence before it to find the other thing that is being compared._ Reread the first sentence. Say: _The sentences are telling us that while some people come to find gold, most people come for other reasons._

COLLABORATE

Have students work in pairs to complete the Leveled Support activities.

Build Meaning Offer language support for the following phrases:

hoped to get rich quickly = wanted to make money quickly

the beauty of the land attracts = the beautiful landscape brings

drew people = brought people to the area

opening stores = starting a business, such as a store

PRODUCTIVE

Have students work in pairs to use one of the phrases in a sentence.

ACADEMIC VOCABULARY

eventually

decline

skilled

discover

SPANISH COGNATES

eventualmente

declinar

descubrir

LEVELED SUPPORT

EMERGING Use the sentence frames to use the word _however._

_Some students like ____. However, other students like ____._

EXPANDING Use the sentence frames to use the word _however._

_Some students ____. However, other ____._

BRIDGING Have students write two sentences using the word _however._

Pages 48–55

ACADEMIC VOCABULARY

determine

series

extend

rise

SPANISH COGNATES

determinar

serie

extenderse

Research Companion, pages 48-55

Teach Academic Vocabulary Write the chart below on the board. Say each word aloud and have students repeat it after you. For Spanish speakers, point out the cognates.

Word	Part of Speech	Definition
determine	noun	control what will happen
series	noun	related things, one coming after another
extend	verb	reach; continue
rise	verb	become higher

Ask: *Who determines what we will do in class every day?* Show students the painting on page 49 of the text. Say: *This is a series of mountain ranges called the Coast Ranges. They extend for 400 miles in the western part of California. Their highest peak rises to about 6,000 feet.*

Vocabulary Word Game: Bean Bag Twister

Materials: Twister mat made out of craft paper or sheet of plastic and two bean bags
Directions: Draw six circles in two rows of three each on the "twister mat." Write a vocabulary word on each circle. Review each vocabulary word. Place the "twister mat" on the ground. Select two students to play the game. Have students stand at opposite ends of the mat. Call out a definition. Have each student toss the bag to land on the vocabulary word that you defined.

California's Mountains

Unpack the Text Write the following sentence on the board and read it aloud:

> Eventually the water flows into rivers that carry this water, known as mountain runoff, across the valley below.

Say: *This sentence has a lot of information.* Ask: *What is the subject of the sentence?* Explain that the subject usually comes at the beginning of a sentence. Point out that the subject is *water*. Ask: *What is the verb, or action word?* Explain that *flowed* is the verb. Demonstrate a flowing movement with your hands. Tell students the next part of the sentence explains what happens to the water and where it goes. The words *known as mountain runoff* tell us the name of this flowing water. Say: *Let's rewrite the sentence. We can take out some words to make it easier to understand.*

> After some time, the water goes into rivers that carry the mountain runoff across the valley below.

 PRODUCTIVE Have students work in pairs to write a sentence using the word *eventually*.

Proper and Common Nouns Review proper and common nouns. Explain that nouns are people, places or things. Write the words *proper* and *common* on the board. Ask: *Which names a specific noun? Which names a thing in general?* Explain that proper nouns name common nouns. Remind students that proper nouns begin with uppercase (capital) letters. Draw this chart on the board:

Common Noun	Proper Noun
lake	
mountain range	
peak	
ocean	

 PRODUCTIVE Distribute the graphic organizer to students. Have them complete the Leveled Support activities.

Build Meaning Provide language support for the following phrases:

sea level = where the sea meets the land

volcanic activity = a volcano that has erupted (exploded)

polar regions = the land at or near the North or South Pole

heavy snows = snow that is several inches deep

Inquiry Journal, pages 52–53

Report Your Findings

Demonstrate Understanding Review the **Report Your Findings** task with students.

Think About It Review key vocabulary words. Place students in pairs. Have partners research California mountain communities. Have them write a paragraph that describes the similarities and differences in these communities.

Write About It Have partners write how mountain communities have changed over time. Have them use facts from their research showing similarities and differences to support their responses. Provide assistance with vocabulary, pronunciation, and idea formation as needed. During the writing task, monitor and offer support as need.

Talk About It Have partners share their responses. Be sure partners explain the similarities and differences that they used in their writing.

Connect to the Essential Question Have partners think about how geography affects communities in California. Have them think of some advantages and disadvantages of living in a mountain community.

Take Action

Project Wrap-Up Review the **Tips for Presenting** with students and check for understanding. Explain any unfamiliar terms and vocabulary. Provide support as needed as students complete the **Project Rubric** and **Project Reflection**.

GRAPHIC ORGANIZER

LEVELED SUPPORT

EMERGING Have students work as a group to skim the text to find a proper noun for each common noun.

EXPANDING/ BRIDGING Have partners do the task above. Then have them write their nouns on the graphic organizer, and then share their nouns with the class.

 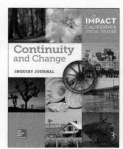

Pages 52–53

How Have California Indians Influenced the Local Region?

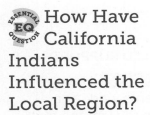

Pages 62–65

SPANISH COGNATES

constitución

cultura

explorador

migrar

misión

nómada

reservación

tradiciones

vegetación

Inquiry Journal, pages 62–65

Introduce the Chapter

Access Prior Knowledge Read the Essential Question aloud to students. Write the words *California Indians* on the board. Find out if students have heard or read about them. Ask: *Have you ever seen California Indian art in a book or at a museum?* Explain that California Indians were the first people to live in the state. Tell students that California Indians influenced the local region. One big influence was the way they used the land. Explain that people still use some of their knowledge and methods today.

Research Questions Have students brainstorm in pairs "just right" research questions (neither too general nor too specific). Use examples and sentence frames to help them form questions:

"How did the California Indians live?" is **too general** because _____.	it has too many answers
"Where did the coastal Indians get their food?" is **too specific** because _____.	it has only one easy answer
"How did the California Indians use the resources in their regions?" is **just right** because _____.	it has more than one answer, but not too many answers

Inquiry Project Help students understand the project they will complete at the end of the chapter. Review any vocabulary that they don't understand, such as *website, assign, determine,* and *conduct.*

Word Rater Remind students that they will learn the meaning of these important words as they read through the chapter. They will make notes each time they learn something new about the word's meaning. Point out the cognates to Spanish speakers. Help them rate the words according to whether they "Know it," "Heard it," or "Don't know it."

Research Companion, pages 58–63

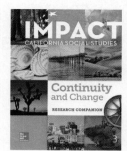

Pages 58–63

Where Do You See California Indian Influence Today? Ask questions about any unfamiliar vocabulary words. Explain that the word *influence* means "the power or action that one person or group has over another." Point out that the way California Indians lived long ago *influenced* the lives of people today.

Write the following sentence on the board and read it aloud:

California Indians created beautiful baskets and pottery.

Ask students to guess what the California Indians might have put in the basket. (nuts, eggs, fruit) Discuss the photograph of the people in the boat. Remind students that California Indians are very much part of modern California. Ask: *Do you know any California Indians?* If students say yes, invite them to share a little about the people.

Connect Through Literature Explain that *The Basket Weaver* is a folktale, a traditional story. Tell students that folktales have some common features. They often begin with a time phrase that tells when the events of the story occurred. This story begins with the words *Thousands of years ago.* Point out that this story tells about Indian life a long time ago. Say: *This story contains many descriptive sentences. Remember, descriptive language helps us form pictures of the characters and action of the story in our minds as we read.*

Write the following sentence on the board and read it aloud:

Her hands moved gracefully, like the wings of a bird.

Point out that sentences that use the word *like* to compare two things are called similes. Similes are a type of descriptive language. Explain that the author uses a simile to describe an action. Ask: *What two things is the author comparing?* Underline the words *hands* and *wings*. Say: *The writer compares Grandmother's hands to the graceful movement of a bird's wings.*

Explain some words and phrases in the story:

in the valley Aw'hay = the name for a low area of land that has steep sides

weaving a basket = making a basket by crossing reeds over and under each other

juncus rushes = leaves from a special plant that grows by the river

soak in mud = covered the reeds in mud

chief = the leader of the tribe or village

feast = a special meal at a festival

blue scrub jay = a kind of bird that has blue feathers

featherless = had no feathers

impressed by her handiwork = amazed by what she had made

twinkled = were bright and happy

COLLABORATE
Have students work in pairs to complete the Leveled Support activities.

Who Lived in Early California?

CONTENT OBJECTIVES

- Explore the lives of American Indians.
- Examine the history and culture of American Indians in California.
- Explain how the lives and culture of American Indians in California have changed over time.

LANGUAGE OBJECTIVES

- Understand the pronoun *they* and its antecedent.
- Analyze a complex sentence.
- Understand the passive voice.
- Identify homophones.

Pages 66–71

SPANISH COGNATES

indígena

historia

antiguo

Inquiry Journal, pages 66–71

Introduce the Lesson

Access Prior Knowledge Before presenting the Lesson Outcomes, read the Lesson Question and find out what students already know about the people who lived in early California. Say: *We have learned about the physical regions of California. These are the areas of land that are made up of mostly one kind of landform.* Tell students that in this lesson, they will study the first people to live in California—the American Indians. Explain that they survived on the natural resources that were available where they lived.

COLLABORATE Have students describe some landforms and regions of California. Ask: *What are the features of each region? How do the features shape industries? What would the early settlers have done in each region?*

Teach Content Vocabulary Write the following chart on the board. Say each word aloud and have students repeat it. For Spanish speakers, point out the cognates.

Word	Part of Speech	Definition
Indians	noun	the people who lived in America before European explorers settled there
history	noun	things that happened in the past
ancient	adjective	from a very long time in the past
homeland	noun	native land; the place where you were born

Ask: *Do you know anything about the <u>history</u> of our city? Can you name any <u>ancient</u> civilizations?* Tell students that another term for <u>Indians</u> is "indigenous people." Ask students to find the two words that make up the compound word <u>homeland</u>. Ask: *How do these words help you understand the meaning of* homeland? If any students were born in another country, ask them to name their *homeland*.

COLLABORATE Have students write sentences using each of the words in the chart.

Analyze the Source

Teach Academic Vocabulary Write the chart below on the board. Say each word aloud and have students repeat it. For Spanish speakers, point out the cognates.

Word	Part of Speech	Definition
explanation	noun	the reasons that someone gives to make something easy to understand
gather	verb	collect
influence	verb	affect
factor	noun	something that has an effect on something else

Point out to students that *explanation* is the noun form of the verb *explain*. Find the words in the Inquiry Journal and discuss what each word means in context. Tell students that they will use these words in their other subjects. Help them find connections with science, math, music, art, health, or physical education. For example, a coach might give an *explanation* of the rules of a game; a scientist *gathers* information before doing an experiment; a famous artist *influences* a young artist; not getting enough sleep may be a *factor* in getting sick.

COLLABORATE

Have students work in pairs to create sentences using various forms of the words *gather* and *influence* (*gather* (v), *gatherer* (n), *be gathering* (v), *gathering* (n), *influence* (v), *influence* (n), *be influencing* (v).

Many Cultures

Unpack the Text Write the following sentence on the board and read it aloud:

> The culture of each group was shaped by the environment of the region they lived in.

First, check that students understand the vocabulary and clarify the meaning of words as needed. Say: *This is a very long sentence. Let's break it up into four parts to find out what it means.* Underline *The culture of each group.* Ask: *What group?* Say: *Let's look at the sentences before to find out. They talk about the different groups of California Indians.* Circle the words *was shaped by.* Say: *The word* shaped *is a verb that means* affected, changed, *or* influenced. Ask: *What shaped the culture of California Indians?* Underline *the environment of the region.* Explain that the sentence is telling us that the *environment* shaped the culture of the California Indians. Underline *they lived in.* Ask: *Who is the pronoun* they *referring to here?* Draw an arrow from *they* to *each group.* Explain that *they* refers to the people in the group who lived in the region.

Explain to students that this sentence is written in the passive voice. Say: *We can rewrite the sentence in the active voice.* Write the following sentence on the board:

> The environment of the region each group lived in shaped their culture.

Explain that the sentence is written in the passive voice because the subject, or main focus, of the sentence is the *culture*, rather than the *environment*.

ACADEMIC VOCABULARY

explanation

gather

influence

factor

SPANISH COGNATES

influencia

factor

Pages 64–71

ACADEMIC VOCABULARY

permanent

convert

support

require

SPANISH COGNATES

permanente

convertir

requerir

LEVELED SUPPORT

EMERGING Have students draw a picture to illustrate one of the meanings of *support*. Then write a caption such as: *My friends supported me when I ran the race.*

EXPANDING / BRIDGING Have students create a role-play for one or more of the meanings of *support*.

Research Companion, pages 64–71

Teach Academic Vocabulary Write the chart below on the board. Say each word aloud and have students repeat it. For Spanish speakers, point out the cognates.

Word	Part of Speech	Definition
permanent	adjective	lasting forever (or a very long time)
convert	verb	change (to a new religion)
support	verb	give help
require	verb	make something necessary

Explain that the word *support* has many meanings. The text in the section "Europeans Bring Change" describes how the Indians had to work to help pay for the cost of the Spanish missions. *Support* also means "to agree with an idea" (*I support her idea*); "hold the weight of something" (*the table legs support the table top*); and "like and follow" (*I support the Golden State Warriors basketball team*). Point out that when you are *required* to do something, you have to do it. For example: *The team is required to practice every Monday.*

 COLLABORATE Have students work in pairs to complete the Leveled Support activities. Check their work for any errors.

Learning About the Past

Unpack the Text Write the following sentence on the board and read it aloud:

> The Chumash fished and hunted sea mammals from canoes made out of trees.

Explain that this sentence has two parts. The first part explains what the Chumash did, and the second part explains how they did it. Underline: *The Chumash fished and hunted sea mammals.* Say: *There are two actions described in the first part of the sentence. What is one thing the Chumash did?* Elicit *They fished.* Then ask: *What is the other thing they did?* Elicit *They hunted sea mammals.* Name some sea mammals, such as seals and whales.

Underline the second part of the sentence. Say: *The Chumash fished and hunted sea mammals. How did they do this? Look at the phrase "from canoes made out of trees."* Explain that the Chumash rode their canoes into the water and fished and hunted from the canoes, and these canoes were made from trees. Say: *We can unpack the sentence into four separate sentences:*

> The Chumash fished.
> The Chumash hunted sea mammals.
> The Chumash used canoes to fish and hunt sea mammals.
> Their canoes were made from trees.

Build Meaning Offer language support for the following phrases:

passed down = gave something to someone who is younger

from one generation to another = from parents to children

hold special festivals = have special events, like dances, ceremonies, or performances

Homophones Review homophones with students. Draw the chart below on the board and write *know* and *no* in the first row. Point out that the words sound alike, but are spelled differently. Demonstrate how both words are used. Say: *If I* know *something, it means I have learned it. If I say* no, *it means I don't agree with something or I don't want to do it.* Point out the silent *k* in *know* and *knew*, and the *-ow* spelling for the long *-o* sound. Then write the rest of the words in the first column. Support students as they complete the second column, as needed.

GRAPHIC ORGANIZER

Homophones	
know	no
knew	new
be	bee
two	to / too
four	for
hear	here
maid	made

COLLABORATE

Have students work in pairs to use each meaning in a sentence.

PRODUCTIVE

Have students work in pairs to complete the Leveled Support activities.

LEVELED SUPPORT

EMERGING Have students complete the second column of the chart with a homophone.

EXPANDING / BRIDGING After students have completed the second column, have them choose two homophones and use them in sentences.

Inquiry Journal, pages 72–73

Report Your Findings

Demonstrate Understanding Review the **Report Your Findings** task with students. Refer to **Collaborative Conversations** on page LL13 for additional sentence frames.

Write About It Place students in pairs. Remind them of the Lesson Question: *Who Lived in Early California?* Discuss what influenced the lives of California Indians. Have students use the sentence starters for their writing.

EMERGING We found out that _____.

EXPANDING/BRIDGING The text states that _____.
This influenced _____.

Provide assistance with vocabulary, pronunciation, and idea formation as needed. During the writing task, monitor and offer support with vocabulary, sentence formation, spelling, and mechanics.

Talk About It Have partners read their paragraphs to each other. Have them discuss the factors they wrote about and how these factors influenced the culture of California Indians.

COLLABORATE

Foster interaction by having students of different proficiencies discuss their paragraphs as they answer the Lesson Question.

Connect to the Essential Question Review the Essential Question with students. Ask who lived in early California. How did the regions in which they settled influence their way of life?

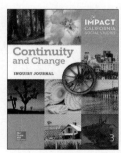

Pages 72–73

How Did the Land Affect California Indians?

CONTENT OBJECTIVES

- Explore how California Indians were affected by their surroundings.
- Examine how California Indians adapted to their surroundings, different climates, and landforms.
- Describe how the daily lives of California Indians in different regions were affected by their environment.

LANGUAGE OBJECTIVES

- Understand the homophones *new* and *knew*.
- Recognize compound words.
- Answer questions in the text.

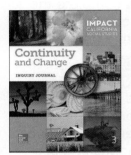

Pages 74–79

SPANISH COGNATES

físico

planta

Inquiry Journal, pages 74–79

Introduce the Lesson

Access Prior Knowledge Read the Lesson Question and access student's prior knowledge about the topic. Encourage them to think about the physical geography of your school's town. Would the terrain make it easy or hard to get around? Is there water nearby? How might the California Indians have used the water (food, transportation, drinking water)? Is it cold or hot, rainy or dry? How do students adapt to the climate? How might the California Indians have adapted to the climate?

Teach Content Vocabulary Write the following chart on the board. Say each word aloud and have students repeat it. For Spanish speakers, point out the cognates.

Word	Part of Speech	Definition
physical	adjective	relating to things you can see and touch; relating to the body
surroundings	noun	the area around you
source	noun	where something comes from
plant	noun	a living thing that grows in soil or water

Elaborate on each word to make connections.

physical: Students may be familiar with the word *physical* from physical education, where it means "relating to the body." *Physical geography* refers to the climate, landforms, and bodies of water in a region.

surroundings: Students have learned the verb *surround*. Help them use their knowledge of the verb form to understand the noun form.

source: Students have seen the word *source* in their Inquiry Journal's "Analyze the Source" section. In that context, *source* means "a place where knowledge comes from," such as a map or an article. In Lesson 2, *source* is used to describe where resources come from, such as a river or a forest.

plant: Have students consider related words from previous lessons, such as *gather*, *field*, *farm*, *crop*, *fertile*, and *rural*.

Analyze the Source

Teach Academic Vocabulary Write the chart below on the board. Say each word aloud and have students repeat it. For Spanish speakers, point out the cognates.

Word	Part of Speech	Definition
daily	adjective/adverb	done every day
inspect	verb	look at closely; examine
retell	verb	tell someone something again
organize	verb	arrange something in a particular way

Explain that the expression _daily_ life refers to the regular things people do every day. Invite students to talk about their own daily lives. How have their surroundings (climate, landforms, resources) influenced their daily lives? Elaborate on the meaning of each word in the context of the Inquiry Journal. When students _inspect_ the map on page 77, what will they do? When they _retell_ information shown on the map, what will they do? When they _organize_ their Inquiry Project Notes on page 81, what will they do?

 COLLABORATE Have students work in pairs to do the Leveled Support activities.

Build Meaning Offer language support for the following phrases:

    widespread = happening over a large area (this is a compound word)

    may have been = version of "may be" refers to things that happened in the past

A Land of Rich Vegetation

Unpack the Text Write the following sentence on the board and read it aloud:

    Each group used what was available in their environment.

First, check that students understand the vocabulary and clarify the meaning of words as needed. Underline the phrase _what was available_. Ask: _What is the word_ what _referring to here? To find out, we have to read the sentences that come before._ Review that these sentences talk about the things the California Indian groups used to make their homes and boats. Say: _We know that in the northern areas they used_ trees _and in the Central Valley they used_ grasses. _That's because trees were available in the northern areas and grasses were available in the Central Valley. So in this sentence_ what _means either trees or grasses, depending on where the groups lived._ We can ask the question:

    What was available in their environment?

The answer is _trees_ (northern areas) or _grasses_ (Central Valley).

ACADEMIC VOCABULARY

daily

inspect

retell

organize

SPANISH COGNATES

inspeccionar

organizar

LEVELED SUPPORT

EMERGING Have students draw a series of pictures showing their daily routine.

EXPANDING / BRIDGING Have partners tell each other about their daily routine. Then switch partners and retell what their original partner said.

Pages 72–77

ACADEMIC VOCABULARY

available

preserve

ceremonial

temporary

SPANISH COGNATES

ceremonial
temporal

Research Companion, pages 72–77

Teach Academic Vocabulary Write the chart below on the board. Say each word aloud and have students repeat it. For Spanish speakers, point out the cognates.

Word	Part of Speech	Definition
available	adjective	easy to use or get
preserve	verb	keep something the same; keep from going bad or being destroyed
ceremonial	adjective	relating to a formal, religious, or cultural event
temporary	adjective	existing or happening for a short time

Discuss each word to further explore its meaning. For example, have students discuss which resources are _available_ in different regions of California, and invite them to share any _ceremonies_ they know about.

COLLABORATE Students have already learned the word _permanent_. Have students work in pairs to make lists of things that are permanent and _temporary_ in order to explore these antonyms more deeply.

Vocabulary Game There are many compound words in Lesson 2: _north/west, shore/line, under/ground, deer/skin, arrow/head, them/selves, some/times, land/form_. Write each word part on a separate index card. Play a game of concentration where students try to match word parts to make a new word. Each time a student makes a match, have them explain what the compound word means.

Build Meaning Offer language support for the following words and phrases:

area that stretched from = all the land from one point to another

as much food as possible = a lot of food; "as much as" is an equivalency, so if you have five fish and you want as much fish as possible, how many fish can you have? (five)

First... Then... Finally = sequence words that tell the reader the order in which things happen

hard to find = hidden or rare

roofs made of brush = We use "made of" to talk about the basic materials or qualities of something. "Brush" in this case means materials from the forest or fields, such as bushes, shrubs, branches, and leaves.

Homophones *new* and *knew* Distribute copies of the graphic organizer to students. Review the definition of the homophones *new* and *knew* with the group.

Have students write a sentence in the column using the correct meaning for the homophones *new* and *knew*.

new	knew

COLLABORATE Have students work in pairs to do the Leveled Support activities.

Adapting to California's Regions

Unpack the Text Write the following sentence (page 77) on the board and read it aloud:

> To protect themselves from the sun, the Chemeheuvi built homes with roofs made of brush.

Ask: *What did the Chemeheuvi do? Which phrase tells you about an action?* Underline and say: *the Chemeheuvi built homes with roofs made of brush.* Ask: *Why did they build homes with roofs made of brush?* Underline and say: *to protect themselves from the sun.*

Examine how this sentence helps students understand the topic. Ask: *What resource did they have?* (brush) *What element of the physical geography did they have to adapt to?* (hot, summer sun) Encourage students to consider these two questions as they continue reading about the California Indians.

Inquiry Journal, pages 80–81

Report Your Findings

Demonstrate Understanding Review the **Report Your Findings** task with students. Refer to **Collaborative Conversations** on page LL13 for additional sentence frames.

Write About It Place students in small groups of three or four. Remind them of the Lesson Question: *How Did the Land Affect California Indians?* Tell them to first gather facts from the text to describe the region and then use that information to explain how the Indians of the region lived.

EMERGING The _____ tribe lived in the _____ region.

They _____.

EXPANDING/BRIDGING In the _____ region, the _____.

Provide assistance with vocabulary, pronunciation, and idea formation as needed. During the writing task, monitor and offer support with vocabulary, sentence formation, spelling, and mechanics.

COLLABORATE Foster interaction by having students of different proficiencies discuss their paragraphs as they answer the Lesson Question.

GRAPHIC ORGANIZER

LEVELED SUPPORT

EMERGING Write several more homophones on the board. Have students use index cards to make flashcards with a word on one side and its homophone on the other. Then they show the flashcard to their partner, who spells the homophone.

EXPANDING / BRIDGING Have students write one sentence with a word from the board and another sentence with its homophone. Then they read each sentence to their partner, who says the correct spelling of the homophones.

 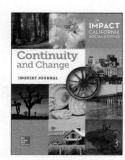

Pages 80–81

How Did California Indians Change the Land?

CONTENT OBJECTIVES

- Explore how and why California Indians changed the land around them.
- Examine how California Indians changed the land around them and how we can learn more about their ways of life.
- Explain why and how the California Indians in your region changed their environment.

LANGUAGE OBJECTIVES

- Locate key details in the text.
- Distinguish sentences from fragments.
- Answer questions in the text.

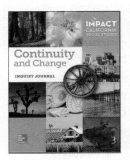

Pages 82–87

Inquiry Journal, pages 82–87

Introduce the Lesson

Access Prior Knowledge Before presenting the Lesson Outcomes, read the Lesson Question and find out what students already know about how human activity changes the land. Discuss your own town. How have humans changed the land? Elicit ideas like the following: forests were cut down to make way for farms, fields, or city streets; dams changed the flow or direction of rivers; tunnels were cut through mountains; roads were paved; concrete was poured to make sidewalks, covering the earth beneath; harbors were built that changed the coastline.

 COLLABORATE Have students discuss how they think California Indians might have adapted to the land and changed the land to survive.

Teach Content Vocabulary Write the following chart on the board. Say each word aloud and have students repeat it. For Spanish speakers, point out the cognates.

Word	Part of Speech	Definition
dam	noun / verb	a strong wall built across a river to stop or slow the water / build such a wall
space	noun	an empty area
forest fire	noun	a fire in a wooded area; some forest fires happen naturally, some happen by accident, and some are started on purpose
medicine	noun	a substance used to cure an illness or injury

Explain that California Indians did some things to change the land. They built _dams_ to make it easier to catch fish. They started _forest fires_ to clear _space_ to grow plants. They used the plants for food and _medicine_.

 PRODUCTIVE Have students work in pairs to complete the Leveled Support activities.

SPANISH COGNATES

espacio

medicina

LEVELED SUPPORT

EMERGING Have students create illustrations of the words. Then have them write a caption for their partner's picture.

EXPANDING / BRIDGING Have students write a sentence with each word, and then read their partner's sentences aloud.

Analyze the Source

Teach Academic Vocabulary Write the chart below on the board. Say each word aloud and have students repeat it. For Spanish speakers, point out the cognates.

Word	Part of Speech	Definition
certain	adjective	particular things, but not saying which ones
guide	verb / noun	help someone or something go somewhere / a person or thing that acts as a guide
clue	noun	information that helps you find an answer
event	noun	something that happens, especially something important or unusual

Ask: *If you want to figure out the meaning of a word, what are some <u>clues</u> you can use?* Explain that clues can <u>guide</u> us to understanding new words and new information. Ask: *Can you think of an important <u>event</u> that happened this year? Is a <u>certain</u> day of the week your favorite? If so, which one?*

Build Meaning Offer language support for the following phrases:

work better = be more productive and useful

cleared the land = cut down the trees and removed the brush to make a field

slow down = make something move more slowly

washed away the soil = the water took the soil away

Working with the Land

Unpack the Text Write the following sentence on the board and read it aloud:

> The Kumeyaay have lived in what is now San Diego County for thousands of years.

Say: *This is a long sentence with a lot of information. Let's break it into parts to find out what it means.* Underline *The Kumeyaay have lived.* Explain that when you see *have* as a helping verb in front of another verb, you know that the two verbs together describe an action that started in the past and continues in the present. So, the Kumeyaay lived in San Diego County thousands of years ago, and they still live there today. Say: *I have lived in California for many years. This means I lived in California for many years in the past, and I am living here now.* Underline the words *what is now.* Say: *These words mean that San Diego County was not always called San Diego County. The Europeans named it in the 18th century. San Diego County is the name the area has now.* Underline *for thousands of years.* Explain that this phrase means more than two thousand years and possibly many thousands of years. No one knows exactly how many years the Kumeyaay have lived in the area, but we know they have lived there for a very long time.

SPANISH COGNATES

cierto

guiar

evento

Pages 78–83

ACADEMIC VOCABULARY

energy

tool

remove

control

SPANISH COGNATES

energía

controlar

Research Companion, pages 78–83

Teach Academic Vocabulary Write the chart below on the board. Say each word aloud and have students repeat it. For Spanish speakers, point out the cognates.

Word	Part of Speech	Definition
energy	noun	the power that comes from gas, oil, solar power, or wind power
tool	noun	a device that you use to help you make or fix something
remove	verb	take away
control	verb	make a person, organization, or object do what you want

Ask: *Oil is one kind of energy. What are some other kinds? What are some examples of tools? How can we remove weeds from the ground? When you play soccer, what do you use to control the ball?*

Build Meaning Offer language support for the following phrases:

blast through mountains = use an explosive, like dynamite, to create a path where a mountain is located

cut down forests = *Cut down* means that you cut something and it falls down; in this case, we cut trees in a forest and they fall down.

meet their needs = If you meet someone's needs, you give them something or you do something so that they get what they need.

COLLABORATE

Have students work in pairs to make sentences with the phrases *blast through*, *cut down*, and *meet their needs*.

Modifying the Land

Unpack the Text Write the following sentence on the board and read it aloud:

The traps let water flow but blocked fish.

Underline the word *but*. Say, *What does the word* but *mean in this sentence?* Explain that the word *but* is a transition word. It is used to connect ideas in a single sentence. It is also a word that is used to show a contrast. Point out the contrast in the sentence by circling the words *flow* and *blocked*. Say: *The word* flow *means that the water is moving. The word* blocked *is the opposite. In this sentence, the traps allow the water to move but they stop the fish.*

COLLABORATE

Have students work in groups of three or four to find sentences with the word *but* in the text and describe the information that the word is contrasting.

Sentences and Fragments Review sentences and fragments. Remind students that a sentence is a complete thought with a subject and a verb.

COLLABORATE Distribute copies of the graphic organizer. Have students work in pairs to rewrite the fragments to make them into sentences.

Sentence Fragments	Sentences
by building fishing traps	
California Indian children	
used fire in many ways	

Inquiry Journal, pages 88–89

Report Your Findings

Demonstrate Understanding Review the **Report Your Findings** task with students. Refer to **Collaborative Conversations** on page LL13 for additional sentence frames.

Have students work in pairs to do the Leveled Support activities.

Think About It Review key vocabulary words. Discuss how the California Indians from your region lived long ago. Describe the geography of your area. Answer the following questions: *What is the climate like? What is the physical geography of the land like?*

Write About It Place students in pairs. Remind them of the Lesson Question: *How Did California Indians Change the Land?* Tell students they will be writing a paragraph explaining how the California Indians changed the environment to meet their needs. Tell them to first gather facts from the text. Tell them to include examples of using fire and water to control the environment.

EMERGING From the text, I know that the _____ tribe used _____ to _____.

EXPANDING According to the text, the _____ tribe _____.

BRIDGING Evidence from the text shows _____.

Provide assistance with vocabulary, pronunciation, and idea formation as needed. During the writing task, monitor and offer support with vocabulary, sentence formation, spelling, and mechanics.

COLLABORATE Foster interaction by having students of different proficiencies discuss their paragraphs as they answer the Lesson Question.

LEVELED SUPPORT

EMERGING Identify ways the California Indians changed their environment to make life easier.

EXPANDING/ BRIDGING Have students use the sentence frames to describe how California Indians changed their environment to make life easier.
The Maidu, Miwok, and Ohlone used fire to ____.

The Hupa and the Yurok used weirs to____.

The Chemehuevi and Mojave dug ditches to ____.

Pages 88–89

LESSON QUESTION

How Did California Indians Use Natural Resources?

CONTENT OBJECTIVES

- Explore how California Indians used natural resources.
- Examine how California Indians used resources to understand more about how they lived.
- Identify the types of natural resources used by California Indians and how these resources shaped their lives.

LANGUAGE OBJECTIVES

- Locate key details in the text.
- Use verb + preposition combinations.
- Understand conditional statements.
- Use *when* to connect two parts of a sentence.

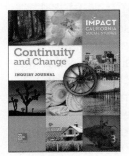

Pages 90–95

SPANISH COGNATES

cotización

transportación

Inquiry Journal, pages 90–95

Introduce the Lesson

Access Prior Knowledge Before presenting the Lesson Outcomes, read the Lesson Question and find out what students already know about how California Indians used natural resources. For example, students may recall that the California Indians changed their environment to make life easier for themselves. Explain to students they will be learning about how California Indians use Natural Resources for things other than survival.

 COLLABORATE Working in pairs, have students describe the natural resources the California Indians had in their regions and how they used them.

Teach Content Vocabulary Write the following chart on the board. Say each word aloud and have students repeat it. For Spanish speakers, point out the cognates.

Word	Part of Speech	Definition
quotation	noun	a sentence or phrase taken from a source, such as a book
elder	noun	someone who is older than you
shelter	noun	a safe place; a home
transportation	noun	vehicles or systems used for getting people or goods from one place to another

Explain that a _quotation_ is the exact words that someone says. Point out that _quotations_ usually have marks around them (" / "). Invite students to name some _elders_ they know, such as grandparents or community leaders. Ask students to describe some _shelters_ they have learned about already in Chapter 2. Remind students that they already learned the verb *transport* and explain that the noun _transportation_ has a related meaning.

 PRODUCTIVE Have students make sentences using each of the vocabulary words.

Analyze the Source

Teach Academic Vocabulary Write the chart below on the board. Say each word aloud and have students repeat it. For Spanish speakers, point out the cognates.

Word	Part of Speech	Definition
image	noun	picture, illustration, map or other visual feature
evidence	noun	something that proves a point or convinces you that something is true
depend	verb	rely
local	adjective	relating to an area near you

Have students look through the Inquiry Journal to find <u>images</u> of resources. (plants, fish). Explain that <u>*local*</u> means near where you live. Ask: *What local natural resources do you* <u>*depend*</u> *on? What would your life be like without those resources?* Explain that when you give an opinion, it is helpful to give <u>*evidence*</u> to support your opinion. Say: *When students do well on tests, this is evidence that they are learning.*

 PRODUCTIVE Have students of different proficiency levels work together to make sentences with the words.

Build Meaning Provide language support for the following phrases:

safe to eat = not dangerous to eat

What would this be like...? = This entire section of text deals with an imaginary situation, so the author uses the conditional forms (would, could).

Using Natural Resources

Unpack the Text Write the following sentence on the board and read it aloud:

What if you lived in a place with no stores or restaurants?

Circle *What*. Ask: *What kind of word is this?* Elicit that it is a question word. Review question words: *When, Where, How*, and *Why*. Say: *Every chapter and lesson in this book starts with a question. Usually, they start with one of these words.* Ask: *Is there another way we know this is a question?* Elicit *because there is a question mark at the end.* Explain that not every question is asking for an answer. Point out that this question starts with *What if*. We use *What if* to talk about something in the present or the future that we don't know about or something that might or might not happen. For example, say: *Imagine that you and your friends are planning to play soccer on Saturday. What if it rains? What will you do then? This sentence is asking us to imagine living in a place with no stores or restaurants.* Another way of writing the question is:

If you lived in a place with no stores or restaurants, what would you do?

We use the helping verb *would* to answer questions like this:

I would have to find my food in the environment.

ACADEMIC VOCABULARY

image

evidence

depend

local

SPANISH COGNATES

imagen

depender

LEVELED SUPPORT

EMERGING Have students answer the question: *What if you had a million dollars?* They can use these sentence frames: *I would buy _____. I would go _____.*

EXPANDING / BRIDGING Have each student write three *What if* statements, and then ask them to their partner. Remind them to use the past form of the verb: *What if you <u>had</u> wings?*

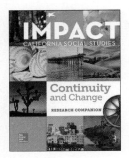

Pages 84–91

ACADEMIC VOCABULARY

belief

visible

decorate

plentiful

SPANISH COGNATES

visible

decorar

Research Companion, pages 84–91

Teach Academic Vocabulary Write the chart below on the board. Say each word aloud and have students repeat it. For Spanish speakers, point out the cognates.

Word	Part of Speech	Definition
belief	noun	an idea that people think is true
visible	adjective	able to be seen
decorate	verb	make something look nicer
plentiful	adjective	having a lot of something available

Point out that _beliefs_ are the things people believe in, such as religious beliefs. Give examples of some religious beliefs: Christianity, Islam, Judaism, Hinduism. Explain to students that everything we see around us in the classroom is _visible_. Things that we can't see are _invisible_. Point out the prefix _in-_ means "not." Ask: _Are stars visible during the day?_ Ask students to think of ways that people _decorate_ a home—for example, painting, putting art on the walls. Ask: _What kinds of fruit are plentiful in California?_

Vocabulary Word Game: Definition Catch

Materials: magnet, string, ruler, colored paper, paper clips
Directions: Cut paper in the shape of fish and write the definition for each new vocabulary word on each fish. Put a paper clip on each paper fish. Make a small fishing pole using the ruler, string, and a magnet. Students take turns "catching a definition fish." If they correctly identify the vocabulary word that matches the definition, they get to keep the fish. This game can be played in pairs or with several students. For control of error you may write the answer on the back of the fish.

Using Plants and Animals

Unpack the Text Write the following sentence on the board and read it aloud:

> The Miwok men made snowshoes from branches and grapevines when they hunted in the hills during winter.

Explain that this sentence gives us a lot of information. Underline the phrase _The Miwok men made snowshoes from branches and grapevines._ Say: _What did the men make? (snowshoes) And they made them from ___ (branches and grapevines)._ Circle the word _when_ and ask: _When did they make these snowshoes? (when they hunted in the hills during winter)_ Explain that the word _when_ connects the two parts of the sentence.

 Have students write sentences with when using this sentence frame.

     I _____ when I _____.

Verb + preposition Explain that some verbs are often followed by certain prepositions. Review the following list of verb + prepositions with the class. Have students locate the phrases in the text.

surrounded by	hoped for
learned to	used for / to
made from	depend on

Students can search the other sections of the Lesson to find other verb + preposition combinations:

shaped by	influenced by
shopping for	adapted to

COLLABORATE

Have students work in pairs to do the Leveled Support activities.

Inquiry Journal, pages 96–97

Report Your Findings

Demonstrate Understanding Review the **Report Your Findings** task with the students. Refer to **Collaborative Conversations** on page LL13 for additional sentence frames.

Think About It Review key vocabulary words. Discuss what resources were important to the California Indians in their local region. Demonstrate skimming the text to locate information.

Write About It Place students in pairs. Remind them of the Lesson Question: *How Did California Indians Use Natural Resources?* Tell students they will be writing a paragraph explaining how the California Indians used natural resources. Tell them to first gather facts and key details from the text to describe their region and then use that information to explain how the California Indians used these resources.

EMERGING   In ____ region, the ____ tribe used ____.

EXPANDING   Because the ____ region had ____, the tribe ____.

BRIDGING   Because the ____ region had ____, the tribe ____. In addition, ____.

Provide assistance with vocabulary, pronunciation, and idea formation as needed. During the writing task, monitor and offer support with vocabulary, sentence formation, spelling, and mechanics.

COLLABORATE

Foster interaction by having students of different proficiencies discuss their paragraphs as they answer the Lesson Question.

LEVELED SUPPORT

EMERGING Have students write sentences using the frames, and then read them to a partner:
Last year, I learned to ____. This year, I hope for ____. I like to go shopping for ___.

EXPANDING / BRIDGING Have students quiz each other. Student A says a verb. Then student B says the preposition that goes with it. Then have them write sentences with two of the verb + preposition combinations.

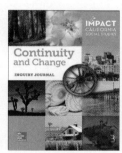

Pages 96–97

What Defines a California Indian Community?

CONTENT OBJECTIVES

- Explore the culture of today's California Indian communities.
- Examine the California Indian communities' impact on California.
- Identify the ways a culture is kept alive and find details that tell about the different California Indian communities.

LANGUAGE OBJECTIVES

- Locate key details in the text.
- Recognize homophones.
- Retell a story sequentially using signal words.
- Recognize pronouns and their antecedents.
- Use prepositions of location in sentences.

Pages 98–103

SPANISH COGNATES

tribu

leyanda

Inquiry Journal, pages 98–103

Introduce the Lesson

Access Prior Knowledge Before presenting the Lesson Outcomes, read the Lesson Question and find out what students already know about factors that help define a community. Invite them to share customs that are popular in your shared school community, or in students' diverse home communities. Tell students that in this lesson they will explore the culture and traditions of California Indians, such as their folklore, music, celebrations, and festivals.

COLLABORATE

 Have students work in pairs to describe how the California Indians changed and adapted to their environments. Have them discuss what they already know about the culture of California Indians.

Teach Content Vocabulary Write the following chart on the board. Say each word aloud and have students repeat it. For Spanish speakers, point out the cognates.

Word	Part of Speech	Definition
tribe	noun	a group of people who live together and share a common culture and language
storyteller	noun	a person who tells stories
legend	noun	a very old story that people tell about an important person or event; sometimes it is not true
foothills	noun	the lower hills next to a mountain or line of mountains

Say: *Indian tribes have a strong tradition of telling stories.* Explain that *storytellers* often tell stories aloud, especially *legends*. Say: *These stories are passed down from adults to children.* Explain that *foothills* are small mountains at the bottom of a bigger mountain or mountain range. Ask students if they can guess why they are called foothills. (The foot is at the bottom of the body; the foothills are at the bottom of larger mountains.)

COLLABORATE

Have students work together to make sentences using each of the words.

Analyze the Source

Teach Academic Vocabulary Write the chart below on the board. Say each word aloud and have students repeat it. For Spanish speakers, point out the cognates.

Word	Part of Speech	Definition
define	noun	describe something clearly
origin	noun	where something begins or comes from
values	noun	beliefs about what is important
purpose	noun	why you do something or why something exists

Explain that the *purpose* of a legend is often to explain the *origin* of something. The legend in the text explains the origin of fire. Another purpose of stories is often to teach people about the *values* of a community, or what is important to the people in the community.

Build Meaning Offer language support for the following phrases:

read aloud = the opposite of *read silently*

stories such as this = stories like this; these types of stories

open grass = an area in a field that doesn't have any trees or protection

put out the fire = "put out" is a two-part verb that means *extinguish*

The Origin of Fire (A Yaudancchi Yokut Legend)

Unpack the Text Write the following sentence on the board and read it aloud:

> He crouched over the fire, holding it in his hands near his belly.

Say: *This is a long sentence with some hard words.* Demonstrate *crouching* for students so they understand the verb. Say: *When you crouch over something, you bend over it like this.* Define *belly*. Say: *A belly is another word for a stomach (point to your stomach). It's an informal or conversational word that we only see in stories.* Circle *He, it, his,* and *his*. Say: *This sentence has a lot of pronouns that replace nouns. To find out who* He *refers to, we need to look at the sentences before.* Point out that the sentences are talking about the jackrabbit. The two possessive pronouns *his* also refer to the jackrabbit. Ask: *What about the pronoun* it? *What does* it *refer to?* Explain that *it* refers to a thing. Draw an arrow from *it* to *the fire*. Say: *The pronoun* it *replaces the fire. Instead of saying* He crouched over the fire, holding the fire in his hands, *we can use a pronoun instead of repeating the noun.*

Review prepositions with students. Underline *over, in,* and *near*. Say: *These three words are called prepositions of location, or place. They tell us where things (the nouns) are.* Demonstrate by putting your hand over, in, and near an object such as a bag.

Point out the comma in the middle of the sentence. Remind students that a comma means a pause or a break in a sentence to separate the actions. Demonstrate by reading the sentence, pausing at the comma.

PRODUCTIVE Have students write sentences using the prepositions *over, in,* and *near*.

Putname, Frederic Ward. "Yaudanchi Yokuts. The Origin of Fire." American Archaeology and Ethnology. Berkeley: Berkeley University Press, 1906-1907.

ACADEMIC VOCABULARY

define

origin

values

purpose

SPANISH COGNATES

definir

origen

valores

propósito

LEVELED SUPPORT

EMERGING Have students draw pictures to illustrate the prepositions *over, in, on,* and *near,* and write a sentence to describe each picture. For example, *The book is* on *the desk.*

EXPANDING / BRIDGING Have students play a guessing game in pairs. One student describes the location of something in the room using prepositions, and the partner guesses the object. For example:
A: *It's on the teacher's desk.* B: *Is it the notebook?* A: *No. It's near her coffee mug.* B: *Is it ____?*

IMPACT
CALIFORNIA SOCIAL STUDIES
Continuity and Change
RESEARCH COMPANION
3

Pages 92–97

ACADEMIC VOCABULARY

trait

custom

employ

common

SPANISH COGNATES

costumbre

emplear

común

Research Companion, pages 92–97

Teach Academic Vocabulary Write the chart below on the board. Say each word aloud and have students repeat it. For Spanish speakers, point out the cognates.

Word	Part of Speech	Definition
trait	noun	a quality or characteristic of someone or something
custom	noun	a way of doing something in a community
employ	verb	give someone work for payment
common	adjective	shared by two or more people or groups

Ask: *What do you think is an important <u>trait</u> of a good grandchild?* (they respect their elders; they are patient; they are kind, etc.) *What are some <u>customs</u> in your family or culture? What companies or organizations in our area <u>employ</u> a lot of people?* Explain that the school system employs their teachers. Ask: *What are some <u>common</u> values that we have at this school?* (kindness, honesty, hard work)

Build Meaning Offer language support for the following phrases:

take part in = participate in something

native language = the first language; the language that a person has known since birth

unusual for (a woman to play) = not typical

perform professionally = to do something as a job

recorded six albums = recorded six collections of songs that go together in one package (albums)

PRODUCTIVE Invite students to name some favorite musicians. Can they name any of their albums? Explain that those artists recorded those albums, just like Mary Youngblood.

Living in Two Worlds

Unpack the Text Write the following sentence on the board and read it aloud:

Many California Indians today split their time between cities and their tribe's reservations.

Underline the words *split their time*. Say: *If you split something, you divide it or cut it in half. Many California Indians live in two places, and they split their time between the two.* Ask: *What are the two places where they live?* (cities and the tribe's reservation).

Invite students to practice this language by filling in a sentence frame with their own information.

[Many students] split their time between [homework] and [playing games].

Homophones Review the homophones *their* and *there*. Draw the following chart on the board to reinforce their meaning:

There	Their
are many California Indians in the valley.	traditions are handed down from generation to generation.

COLLABORATE

Distribute copies of the graphic organizer. Have students work in pairs to do the Leveled Support activities.

Inquiry Journal, pages 104–105

Report Your Findings

Demonstrate Understanding Review the **Report Your Findings** task with students. Refer to **Collaborative Conversations** on page LL13 for additional sentence frames.

Write About It Place students in pairs. Remind them of the Lesson Question: *What Defines a California Indian Community?* Tell students they will be writing a paragraph describing one way in which the California Indian communities continue to share their traditions. Brainstorm some of the specific communities and the different ways they preserve their heritage, such as maintaining traditional customs, using and learning tribal language, and holding special festivals.

EMERGING   The_____ keep their cultures by _____.

EXPANDING/BRIDGING   According to the text, _____. It reveals _____.

Provide assistance with vocabulary, pronunciation, and idea formation as needed. During the writing task, monitor and offer support with vocabulary, sentence formation, spelling, and mechanics.

COLLABORATE

Foster interaction by having students of different proficiencies discuss their paragraphs as they answer the Lesson Question.

GRAPHIC ORGANIZER

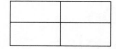

LEVELED SUPPORT

EMERGING On the board, write some sentences with *their* and *there* clozed. Have students write the sentences with the correct homophone in the graphic organizer.

EXPANDING/BRIDGING Have students think of another homophone of *there* and *their* (*they're*). Have students write a sentence with each of the homophones.

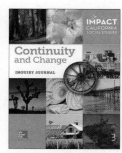

Pages 104–105

How Do California Indian Communities Work?

CONTENT OBJECTIVES

- Explore the economy and government of California's Indian groups.
- Examine the economy and government to understand California Indian communities.
- Describe how many California Indian communities are organized.

LANGUAGE OBJECTIVES

- Understand sentence structure.
- Use the conjunction *or* to write sentences about choices.
- Use *such as* to give examples.
- Understand multiple meaning words.

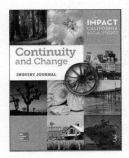

Pages 106–111

SPANISH COGNATES

gobierno

territorio

capitán

Inquiry Journal, pages 106–111

Introduce the Lesson

Access Prior Knowledge Before presenting the Lesson Outcomes, read the Lesson Question and find out what students already know about California Indian communities, their economy, and their government. Ask if anyone has visited a museum and seen Indian art or artifacts. Say: *When groups of people live together, they need to be organized and live by rules.* Ask: *Who helps a group stay organized? How do you think California Indian tribes are organized?*

COLLABORATE Explain to students that they are members of a group. The large group is the school community. That large group is broken up into smaller groups known as classes. Working in pairs, have students discuss how their school group is organized.

Teach Content Vocabulary Write the chart below on the board. Say each word aloud and have students repeat it. For Spanish speakers, point out the cognates.

Word	Part of Speech	Definition
government	noun	a group of people who rule a country
band	noun	a tribe, or group, of people who do live and work together
territory	noun	land that is owned by someone or something
captain	noun	the leader of a team

Say: *The California Indian communities have territory, or land, that is set aside for the tribes to live on.* Explain that the *bands* of Indians have their own *government*. Some tribes have elected *captains* to help make the laws for the group to follow. In other bands, the captains are born into the position.

COLLABORATE Have students work in pairs to write sentences using two of the words. Then have them read each other's sentences aloud.

Analyze the Source

Teach Academic Vocabulary Write the chart below on the board. Say each word aloud and have students repeat it. For Spanish speakers, point out the cognates.

Word	Part of Speech	Definition
council	noun	a group of people who are elected to rule a town
protect	verb	keep someone or something safe
decision	noun	a choice you make
position	noun	the role of a person

Point out that the word _council_ is a noun used to talk about a group of people. A _council_ works together to make _decisions_ for a tribe. There is another word that sounds the same but is spelled differently. That word is _counsel_. It is a verb and means "to give advice." Some schools have workers called _counselors_ who give advice to students. Ask: _What is my position?_ Elicit _teacher_. Say: _Part of my job is to protect you and keep you safe._

COLLABORATE

Have students work in pairs to write sentences using two of the words. Then have them read each other's sentences aloud.

Leading the Kumeyaay

Unpack the Text Write the following sentence on the board and read it aloud:

> Captains might be born into the position, or they might be chosen because they were good leaders.

Review the conjunction _or_ with students. Explain that this sentence tells us two ways that people can become captains in an Indian tribe government. Say: _This sentence explains both ways. The ways, or ideas, are connected by the conjunction,_ or. Remind students that conjunctions are connecting words. Other conjunctions are _and_ and _but_. Explain that the word _or_ gives us a choice. You can do one thing or you can do another thing. Say: _When you see the word_ or _in a sentence, remember it is a word that tells choices. Let's write each choice in its own sentence._

> Captains might be born into the position.

> Captains might be chosen because they were good leaders.

Cross out the word _Captains_ in the second sentence and write _or they_. Point out that we add a comma before _or_ because it comes between two separate sentences.

Build Meaning Offer language support for the following phrases:

natural resources = plants, minerals, soil, animals found on the Earth

in charge = leading, making decisions

food source = where people get their food

PRODUCTIVE

Have students try to use one of the phrases in a sentence.

IMPACT
CALIFORNIA SOCIAL STUDIES

Continuity
and Change

RESEARCH COMPANION

Pages 98–105

ACADEMIC VOCABULARY

trade

document

duty

power

SPANISH COGNATES

document

poder

Research Companion, pages 98–105

Teach Academic Vocabulary Write the chart below on the board. Say each word aloud and have students repeat it. For Spanish speakers, point out the cognates.

Word	Part of Speech	Definition
trade	verb	buy or sell things
document	noun	a paper or book that gives information
duty	noun	a job; something a person has to do
power	noun	the ability to change or control things

Ask: *What kinds of things do people* <u>*trade*</u> *for money?* Elicit the things people buy at stores. *What* <u>*documents*</u> *do people need to travel?* Elicit a passport. *What are your* <u>*duties*</u> *as a member of your family? What* <u>*power*</u> *does your teacher have? What power do you have?*

COLLABORATE Reinforce the concept of how California Indian communities function. Have students work in pairs and use the terms above to describe how these tribes supported themselves.

Vocabulary Word Game: "Hot Potato" Vocabulary Elimination Game

Directions: Write each vocabulary word on an individual index card. Students sit in a circle with a timer set for a random amount of time (3 to 5 minutes). Shuffle the cards and give the deck to the first student in the circle. That student draws a card and tries to get other students to guess the word by giving verbal clues. The student cannot say the word or any part of the word. When someone guesses the word, the student passes the stack to the next student who takes a turn with another word. The student holding the stack of cards when the timer goes off leaves the circle. Continue until only one student is remaining.

Money and Trade

Unpack the Text Write the following sentence on the board and read it aloud:

> They traded the goods they made such as canoes and clothes for goods and resources they needed.

Underline the words *such as*. Say: *This sentence tells us information about the things that California Indians traded.* Explain that the sentence wants to provide more information by giving examples. Say: *The sentence gives two examples. We use the words* such as *when we give examples. The examples are connected by the word* and. *We can rewrite the sentence another way by using* For example.

> They traded goods they made. For example, they traded canoes and clothes for goods and resources.

Cross out the words *For example, they traded* and write *such as*. Explain that we can connect the two sentences using *such as*.

PRODUCTIVE Have students work in pairs to write a sentence that gives examples using the words *such as*.

Multiple Meaning Words Review with students that some words have more than one meaning. Review the two meanings of the word *band*. Write the meanings on the board and discuss each meaning. Explain that both meanings refer to a group of people. However, one group plays music. The other refers to Indian communities.

Definition 1	Definition 2
Indian communities	a group that plays music

 Distribute the graphic organizer to students. Have them write the definitions on two pieces of paper. When you say each of the sentences shown in the Leveled Support activities, have students hold up the correct definition of *band*.

Build Meaning Provide language support for the following phrases:

shorter strands = small strings of beads

provide services = give help or do a job

in charge of leading = has the job of taking care of people

collecting taxes = getting money from people for taxes

administer justice = keep things fair

independent = not relying on anything else

create new legislation = make new laws

was appointed = was given the job

Inquiry Journal, pages 112–113

Report Your Findings

Demonstrate Understanding Review the **Report Your Findings** task with students.

Think About It Review key vocabulary words. Place students in pairs. Have partners research why California Indians still have their own government today. Have them write a paragraph that explains why California Indians still have their own governments.

Write About It Have partners write a paragraph that explains how California Indian governments are organized. Provide assistance with vocabulary, pronunciation, and idea formation as needed. During the writing task, monitor and offer support as need.

Talk About It Have partners share their response. Be sure partners discuss how California Indian governments work today and what services they provide for their people.

Connect to the Essential Question Have partners think about why it is important to learn about the organization of California Indians.

Take Action

Project Wrap-Up Review the **Tips for Presenting** with students and check for understanding. Explain any unfamiliar terms and vocabulary. Provide support as needed as students completed the **Project Rubric** and **Project Reflection**.

GRAPHIC ORGANIZER

LEVELED SUPPORT

EMERGING Say:
1. *Each band has its own land.*
2. *My brother plays the guitar in a band.*

EXPANDING/BRIDGING
Say:
1. *A band could have 200 people or as many as 1,000 people.*
2. *Our school band practiced for the spring festival.*

Pages 112–113

How and Why Communities Change Over Time

EQ
How Has Life Changed for People in My Community Over Time?

Lesson 1
Communities Grow and Change

Lesson 2
Newcomers Bring Changes

Lesson 3
Communities Then and Now

Lesson 4
Changing Environments

Lesson 5
Community History

Lesson 6
Special Places

Pages 116–119

SPANISH COGNATES

acueducto

década

grupo étnico

expedición

innovación

Inquiry Journal, pages 116–119

Introduce the Chapter

Access Prior Knowledge Read the Essential Question aloud to students. Discuss how life changes over time, or a period of many years. Ask: *How has your life changed since you were born?* Point out that just like people, communities can change over time, too. Give some examples for discussion, such as new housing developments or office buildings being built in the community, or parks and waterfront areas being improved or restored.

Research Questions Have students brainstorm in pairs "just right" research questions (neither too general nor too specific). Use examples and sentence frames to help them form questions:

"How do communities grow and change?" is **too general** because_____.	there are too many answers
"Is the new park good for the community?" is **too specific** because _____.	there is only one easy answer
"What changes have had the biggest impact on your community?" is **just right** because _____.	there is more than one answer, but not too many answers

Inquiry Project Help students understand the project they will complete at the end of the chapter. Review any vocabulary that they don't understand, such as *sequence*, *role*, *growth*, *locations*, and *images*.

Word Rater Remind students that they will learn the meaning of these important words as they read through the chapter. They will make notes each time they learn something new about the word's meaning. Point out the cognates to Spanish speakers. Help them rate the words according to whether they "Know it," "Heard it," or "Don't know it."

Pages 108–113

How Has Life in Communities Changes? Ask questions about any unfamiliar vocabulary words. Explain that the word *inventions* means "new things that were made developed," such as a machine or a new way of farming. Point out that since the 1800s life has changed a lot because of new inventions.

Read the following sentences aloud:

> Early settlers were happy when they could use a hand-powered pump to pump water directly into their houses.

Circle both of the words *pump*. Explain that we can use *pump* as a noun or a verb. Point out that the reader must look at how the word is used in the context of the sentence to tell if the word is an object (noun) or an action (verb). Say: *The context, or the words and sentences that come before and after a word, can help us figure out its meaning.* Ask students to tell which *pump* is a noun and which is a verb.

Connect Through Literature Explain that *Visions of Urban California* is a nonfiction article. Make sure students understand that *urban California* means *city life in California*. Tell students the information contained in the article is true, and you can look up the facts. Explain that this article contains a lot of information. Write this sentence on the board and read it aloud:

> California's early painters liked to paint landscapes showing the state's spectacular natural beauty.

Explain that an author chooses a theme, or main idea, for an article. Say: *This is the main idea the author wanted to discuss in the article.*

Write these sentences on the board and read them aloud:

> At this time, many artists turned away from pretty landscapes. They began painting scenes of everyday urban life, or the "American Scene."

Point out the author is explaining how artists' styles have changed over time. Explain that *turned away* is a phrasal verb. The adverb *away* changes or adds to the meaning of the verb *turn*. To *turn away* from something means to stop doing it. Say: *The author tells us that the style of painting changed during the 1930s, just as people and communities change over time.*

Explain some of the words and phrases in the article:

master = someone who does something extremely well

candid photographs = photographs taken without people knowing they are being photographed

flattering view = a good-looking view

Great Depression = a time when there was much economic hardship

skyscrapers = ver tall buildings

brilliant sunshine = very bright sunshine

COLLABORATE Have students work in pairs to complete the Leveled Support activities.

LESSON QUESTION

Why Do People Move to a New Region?

CONTENT OBJECTIVES

- Explore why people move to a new region.
- Explain the reasons people have moved to a new place by reading and talking about people who have moved to a new region.
- Explain the main reasons people move to a new place or stay where they are.

LANGUAGE OBJECTIVES

- Identify the subject of a sentence.
- Ask *Wh-* questions to understand the information in a sentence.
- Recognize and use noun phrases.
- Identify and use action verbs.

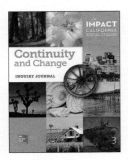

Pages 120–125

SPANISH COGNATES

desastre

educación

tecnología

Inquiry Journal, pages 120–125

Introduce the Lesson

Access Prior Knowledge Before presenting the Lesson Outcomes, read the Lesson Question and find out what students already know about why people move to a new region. Ask: *What are some of the things you like about living in California?* Point out that the climate is one reason many people want to live in this region. Say: *Another reason people move to a region is to find work.* Ask: *What kinds of jobs bring people to California?*

COLLABORATE Have students work in pairs to explain why the climate in their region would attract people to move to the state. Have them share their ideas with the group.

Teach Content Vocabulary Write the chart below on the board. Say the words aloud and have students repeat them after you. For Spanish speakers, point out the cognates.

Word	Part of Speech	Definition
disaster	noun	something that causes a lot of harm or damage
pollute	verb	make water, air, or the ground dirty
education	noun	the process of teaching and learning in a school
technology	noun	machines or devices created by using science and engineering

Ask questions to check understanding: *Can you name a kind of natural <u>disaster</u>? What are some things that <u>pollute</u> our air and water? Why is it important to get a good <u>education</u>?* Say: *Computer <u>technology</u> has changed the way we talk to each other and learn new things.*

COLLABORATE Have students work in pairs to write sentences using the words.

Analyze the Source

Teach Academic Vocabulary Write the chart below on the board. Say each word aloud and have students repeat it. For Spanish speakers, point out the cognates.

Word	Part of Speech	Definition
migrate	verb	move from one place to live in another place
state	verb	say or write something very clearly
trace	verb	follow something, such as a line
label	noun	a word or phrase that describes something

Ask questions to check understanding: *What do you think are some reasons people have migrated to California?* Say: *When you look at a graph, be sure to read the labels. They give you important information about the graph. When we trace something, we follow its lines carefully to make a copy.*

Build Meaning Offer language support for these phrases in the text:

> **military bases** = places where soldiers live and work

> **center of the technology industry** = place where lots of technology is created

California, Here We Come!

Unpack the Text Write the following sentence on the board and read it aloud:

> After the war ended, many of these people stayed in California.

Explain to students that a sentence often, but not always, starts with the subject of the sentence—that is, *who* or *what* the sentence is about. In this sentence, however, the subject is not at the beginning of the sentence. Circle the words *After the war ended*. Say: *This sentence starts with a time phrase that tells us* when something happened, *so we need to keep looking for the subject.* Underline *many of these people*. Say: *This noun phrase is the subject of the sentence.* Explain that *these people* refers to the people talked about in the previous sentence: the people who came to California to work on military bases and who came to build airplanes and ships.

Ask: *Now, what did many of these people do?* Elicit the answer *They stayed in California.* Explain that we can move the time phrase of the sentence to the end:

> Many of these people stayed in California after the war ended.

Point out that we include a comma after the time phrase when it appears at the beginning of the sentence. We don't need to include a comma when the phrase is at the end of the sentence.

COLLABORATE Have students work in pairs to do the Leveled Support activities.

ACADEMIC VOCABULARY

migrate

state

trace

label

SPANISH COGNATES

migrar

traza

LEVELED SUPPORT

EMERGING Have students write a sentence using this frame:

After I started school, I _____.

EXPANDING/ BRIDGING Have students write a sentence using this frame:

After _____, _____.

Pages 114–119

ACADEMIC VOCABULARY

double

precious

expand

seeker

SPANISH COGNATES

doble

precioso

expandir

Research Companion, pages 114–119

Teach Academic Vocabulary   Write the chart below on the board. Say each word aloud and have students repeat it after you. For Spanish speakers, point out the cognates.

Word	Part of Speech	Definition
double	verb	make something two times as much or as many
precious	adjective	rare and expensive
expand	verb	increase in size or number
seeker	noun	a person who is looking for something

Erase the definitions from the board. Ask questions to check understanding: *What do you call someone who is looking for something?* (seeker) *When something increases in size, what does it do?* (expands) *When something is two times as much, what is it?* (double) *Gold and silver objects are what?* (precious)

 Reinforce the concept of why people live and move to a region. Have students work in pairs to explain why some people moved to California.

Build Meaning   Offer language support for the following terms and phrases:

natural disaster = a disaster caused by nature that can destroy life and property

Depression = a time when there are not many jobs

changed over time = changed over many years

strike it rich = make lots of money

the gold soon ran out = there was no more gold

Communities Grow and Change

Unpack the Text   Write the following sentence on the board and read it aloud:

> Other people came to San Francisco to start businesses that sold tools and other things to the miners.

Remind students that the subject often comes at the beginning of a sentence. Point out that in this sentence, the subject is *people* and the word *other* tells us which people. Say: *Let's find out what the sentence is telling us by asking some Wh- questions.* Elicit the answers from students, and underline each part of the sentence as they respond.

Who came? (Other people)

Where did they come to? (San Francisco)

Why did they come? (to start businesses)

What did they sell? (tools and other things)

Who did they sell to? (the miners)

Say: *Now we know why other people came to San Francisco and what they did.*

Action Verbs Remind students that there are different kinds of verbs. One kind of verb are action verbs. Say: *An action verb is a word that tells us what the subject of the sentence is doing or did in the past. For example: I walk to school every day. We played basketball yesterday.*

Draw the chart below on the board. Say: *The text has lots of action verbs. Let's skim the text to find these verbs.* Have students search for action verbs. Model the process of filling in the chart.

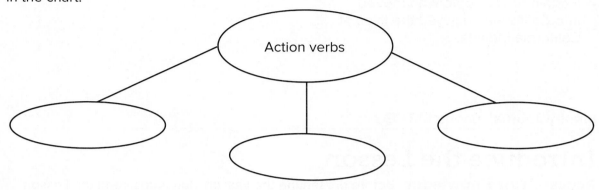

(Possible answers: *move, migrate, travel, dock, settled, dug, looking, building, created, used, discovered, grew, reached, polluted*)

COLLABORATE Distribute the graphic organizer to students. Have students work in pairs to complete the Leveled Support activities. Check their work for any errors.

Inquiry Journal, pages 126–127

Report Your Findings

Demonstrate Understanding Review the **Report Your Findings** task with students.

Think About It Review key vocabulary words. Ask students to think why people migrate to a new place.

Write About It Place students in pairs. Ask students to write about the main reason people might migrate to a new place. Have them explain their choice.

EMERGING	I think people migrated because _____.
EXPANDING	For example, _____.
BRIDGING	According to the text, _____.

Provide assistance with vocabulary, pronunciation, and idea formation as needed. During the writing task, monitor and offer support with vocabulary, sentence formation, spelling, and mechanics.

Talk About It Ask partners to compare choices and explain them. Discuss why people often have more than one reason for moving.

COLLABORATE Foster interaction by having students of different proficiencies discuss their opinions and the supporting reasons as they answer the Lesson Question.

Connect to the Essential Question Ask students to write about how and why communities change over time.

LEVELED SUPPORT

EMERGING Have students write three action verbs from the text in the graphic organizer.

EXPANDING/ BRIDGING After students have completed the graphic organizer, have them work together to use the verbs in another sentence.

Pages 126–127

How Did Settlers and California Indians Interact?

CONTENT OBJECTIVES

- Explore how European and American settlers lived with California Indians.
- Explain how California was settled and what happened to California Indian communities over time.
- Explain how people who moved into California changed the lives of California Indians.

LANGUAGE OBJECTIVES

- Identify multiple-meaning words.
- Recognize possessive pronouns.
- Understand how to form possessives with nouns.

Pages 128–133

SPANISH COGNATES

cultura

religión

Inquiry Journal, pages 128–133

Introduce the Lesson

Access Prior Knowledge Before presenting the Lesson Outcomes, read the Lesson Question and find out what students already know about how European and American settlers treated Native Americans. Remind students that the California Indians had lived in the region for a very long time. Ask: *How do you think the California Indians felt when many new people arrived and settled their lands?* Point out that the cultures and ways of life of the groups of people were very different.

COLLABORATE Working in pairs, have students explain why European and American settlers and California Indians might have had differences. Have them share their ideas with the group.

Teach Content Vocabulary Write the chart below on the board. Say the words aloud and have students repeat them after you. For Spanish speakers, point out the cognates.

Word	Part of Speech	Definition
newcomers	noun	people who have recently arrived in a place
culture	noun	the way a group of people in a particular place speak, act, eat, and dress
missionary	noun	a person who goes to another country or region to teach people about religion
religion	noun	a system of beliefs used to worship a god or gods

Say: *Newcomers are people who have moved to a new place. The newcomers to California wanted the California Indians to change their culture. They wanted the Indians to speak and dress like Americans. Some of the newcomers were missionaries. They wanted the Indians to change their religion.*

COLLABORATE Have students work in pairs to write sentences using the words.

Analyze the Source

Teach Academic Vocabulary Write the chart below on the board. Say each word aloud and have students repeat it. For Spanish spakers, point out the cognates.

Word	Part of Speech	Definition
similar	adjective	almost the same as something else
interact	verb	communicate with other people
claim	verb	say that something belongs to you
gain	verb	get something useful

Explain that the word *similar* means that two or more things are almost alike or the same. Say: *How are we similar to each other? How are we different?* Point out that in school, students *interact* with each other and with the teacher. Point out that the word *claim* has two meanings. Explain that one meaning is to say that something is true. The other meaning is to say that something, such as land, belongs to you. Say: *We often use the word gain with the word control. If you gain control of someone or something, you get power over it.*

Build Meaning Offer language support for the following phrases in the text:

way of life = how people live

in what is now = in a place that today has a different name

A Clash of Cultures

Unpack the Text Write the following sentences on the board and read them aloud:

> The Spanish expected the Indians to live on the mission. They expected them to change their religion.

Circle *They* and *them*. Explain that these are two pronouns—words that take the place of nouns. Both pronouns are plural. Ask: *How can we tell who these pronouns refer to?* Explain that the way the writer has structured the sentences helps us.

Say: *Let's read the first sentence again. Who are the people in this sentence?* Elicit *the Spanish* and *the Indians*. Ask: *Who is the sentence about?* Explain that *The Spanish* are the subject of the sentence. We know this because of the verb *expected*. Say: *Look at the second sentence. It has the same verb,* expected. *So, we know that* They *refers to the Spanish, and* them *refers to the Indians.* Draw an arrow from *They* to Spanish and from *them* to *Indians*.

Underline *their religion*. Say: *The word* their *is a possessive pronoun. It means the religion belonged to someone. Who did it belong to?* Point out that to answer this question, we can ask: *What did the Spanish expect the Indians to do?* The answer is they wanted the Indians to change their religion.

ACADEMIC VOCABULARY

similar

interact

claim

gain

SPANISH COGNATE

similar

interactuar

ganar

LEVELED SUPPORT

EMERGING Have students complete the sentence starters:

People who arrive in a new place today are called _____.

People who arrived in a new place many years ago are called _____.

EXPANDING/ BRIDGING Have students work in pairs to use the academic words in sentences. Then ask them to share their sentences with the group.

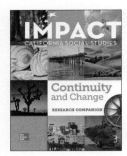

Pages 120–127

ACADEMIC VOCABULARY

found

conflict

specific

recover

SPANISH COGNATES

fundar

conflicto

específico

Research Companion, pages 120–127

Teach Academic Vocabulary Write the chart below on the board. Say each word aloud and have students repeat it. For Spanish speakers, point out the cognates.

Word	Part of Speech	Definition
found	verb	create something that will exist for a long time
conflict	noun	disagreements or fights between groups
specific	adjective	particular; one among many
recover	verb	become well again after you are sick or injured

Say: *Found is the past tense of find. It also has another meaning: to create something, like a city, country, or company.* Say: *There was conflict between the newcomers and the California Indians.* Ask: *What are some specific conflicts that you sometimes have with other people?* Ask: *If you are sick, what can help you recover?*

 Have students work in pairs to write sentences with the words.

Build Meaning Provide language support for the following phrases:

as time went by = as time passed

claimed the land = said the land belonged to you

taking over = being in control

Vocabulary Word Game: Pantomime Verb Game

Materials: Action verbs written on small cards
Directions: Place a stack of vocabulary words with verbs written on small cards face down in the center of the circle. Have pairs of students select a card and pantomime the action. The student that guesses the action is the next one to draw a card and pantomime the action with a partner.

Spanish Explorers Arrive in the Americas

Unpack the Text Write the following sentence on the board and read it aloud:

In 1492, Christopher Columbus sailed from Spain to find a way to travel to Asia across the Atlantic Ocean.

Say: *This sentence has a lot of information. Let's look at it closely so we can understand it better. First, let's find the subject of the sentence.* Ask: *What is the subject?* Remind students that the subject often comes at the beginning of a sentence. Point out that in this sentence, the subject is *Christoper Columbus.* Ask: *Now, what is the first verb, or action word, in the sentence?* Elicit *sailed.*

Remind students that asking *Wh-* questions can help us find information the sentence. Ask: *Who sailed?* (Christopher Columbus) *Why did Christopher Columbus sail?* (to find a way to travel to Asia) Say: *The next part explains the way Columbus traveled. Who can tell me what that way was?* Elicit *across the Atlantic Ocean.* Say: *This sentence tells us where Columbus sailed and why.*

Possessives Review that in English, there are two possible ways to form the possessive: using the word *of* and using an apostrophe before or after the letter *s*. Say: *Where we place the apostrophe depends on whether the noun is singular or plural. When it is singular, we usually put the apostrophe before the* s. *When the word is plural, we usually put the apostrophe after the* s. Write *California Indians' homelands* on the board. Draw the chart on the board. Complete the first two examples from the text:

Owner	Object	Possessive with Apostrophe
California (singular)	coast	California's coast
Students (plural)	discussion	Students' discussion
The teacher (singular)	ideas	
The baby (singular)	toys	
The Indians (plural)	culture	

COLLABORATE

Distribute the graphic organizer to students. Have them complete the Leveled Support activities.

Inquiry Journal, pages 134–135

Report Your Findings

Demonstrate Understanding Review the **Report Your Findings** task with students.

Think About It Review key vocabulary words. Ask students to think about how the lives of the California Indians changed with the arrival of the newcomers.

Write About It Place students in pairs. Ask students to write about the positive and negative things that happened when the different cultures met.

EMERGING A good thing that happened when the Spanish and Indian cultures met was _____. A bad thing that happened was _____.

EXPANDING/BRIDGING According to the text, a positive thing that happened when the Spanish and Indian cultures met was _____. A negative thing that happened was _____.

Provide assistance with vocabulary, pronunciation, and idea formation as needed. During the writing task, monitor and offer support with vocabulary, sentence formation, spelling, and mechanics.

Talk About It Ask partners to discuss their responses. Discuss if the mixing of the cultures had more of a positive or negative effect.

COLLABORATE

Foster interaction by having students of different proficiencies discuss their opinions and the supporting reasons as they answer the Lesson Question.

Connect to the Essential Question Ask students to think about the people and events they read about. How did they change things for California today?

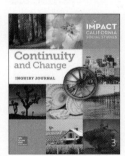

How Do Communities of the Past Compare to Today?

CONTENT OBJECTIVES

- Explore how communities change over time.
- Explain how California was settled and what happened to California Indian communities over time.
- Explain how people who moved into California changed the lives of California Indians.

LANGUAGE OBJECTIVES

- Identify compound sentences.
- Understand a sentence with a noun phrase + *who* and *when* phrases.
- Understand how to form plural nouns by adding *-s*.

Pages 136–141

SPANISH COGNATES

poblácion

transcontinental

economía

Inquiry Journal, pages 136–141

Introduce the Lesson

Access Prior Knowledge Before presenting the Lesson Outcomes, read the Lesson Question and find out what students already know about how communities of the past compare to communities today. Ask, *What is a community*? Elicit that a community is a city or town and the people who live there. Review with students how communities have changed since European and American settlers came. Ask: *What do you remember about California Indian communities? How are they different from our community today?*

 COLLABORATE Have students work in pairs to explain some positive and some negative changes to communities over the years. Have them share their ideas with the group.

Teach Content Vocabulary Write the chart below on the board. Say each word aloud and have students repeat it. For Spanish speakers, point out the cognates.

Word	Part of Speech	Definition
population	noun	all the people who live in a place
background	noun	a person's family and life experience
transcontinental	adjective	crossing a continent
economy	noun	the process of producing, selling and buying goods and services in a country or region

Say: *California is the state with the largest underline{population}. About 39 million people live here. They have many different underline{backgrounds}. Some people were born in California, and many people moved here from different states and countries. Say: underline{Transcontinental} means traveling across a continent. If you make a transcontinental trip from California, where will it end?* (Accept any east coast locations.) Say: *An underline{economy} is the money that a country makes and spends. California has a bigger economy than many countries!*

 COLLABORATE Have students work in pairs to write sentences using the words.

Analyze the Source

Teach Academic Vocabulary Write the chart below on the board. Say each word aloud and have students repeat it. For Spanish speakers, point out the cognates.

Word	Part of Speech	Definition
diverse	adjective	including many different kinds of people or things
influence	noun	the effect somebody/something has on the way someone/something acts
celebrate	verb	do special activities on an important day
recently	adverb	not long ago

Point out that in Chapter 1, students learned the verb *influence*. *Influence* can also be used as a noun. Say: *California is a <u>diverse</u> state. People with many different backgrounds live here. This has an <u>influence</u> on California's culture. People speak many languages and eat many different kinds of food.* Ask: *Have you <u>celebrated</u> any special days <u>recently</u>? Who did you celebrate with? What did you do?*

 COLLABORATE Have students work in pairs to complete the Leveled Support activities.

Build Meaning Offer language support for these terms and phrases in the text.

> **ethnic group** = people of the same culture
>
> **good soil** = dirt that it is easy to grow food in
>
> **made up of** = made by things that were put together

How the Past Can Be Seen Today

Unpack the Text Write the following sentence on the board and read it aloud:

> The way a building looks can tell you who built it and when it was built.

Say: *Let's look closely at the sentence so we can understand the meaning.* Circle the words *who* and *when*. Say: *Who and when are question words.* Ask: *What does the word when ask about?* Elicit that *when* asks about time. Ask: *What does the word who ask about?* Elicit that *who* asks about a person. Underline the noun phrase *The way a building looks*. Point out to students that we can say this another way: *How a building looks* or *What a building looks like*. Ask: *What can we learn by looking at a building?* Elicit that we can learn who built it and when people built it. Explain that the sentence means *When we look at a building, we can learn something about the people who built it. We can also get information about when people built it.*

 PRODUCTIVE Have students work in pairs to write a sentence using either the word *who* or *when*.

Lesson 3 **65**

ACADEMIC VOCABULARY

diverse

influence

celebrate

recently

SPANISH COGNATES

diverso

influencia

celebrar

recientemente

LEVELED SUPPORT

EMERGING Have students list a few ways in which their city or town is diverse (*e.g., people, food, buildings*).

EXPANDING Have students write a sentence with each academic word and then read each other's sentences aloud.

BRIDGING Have students think of different forms of two of the words, and write sentences with their partner's words. Examples: *celebration, diversity, influential*.

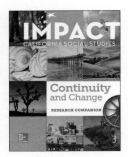

Pages 128–137

ACADEMIC VOCABULARY

destination

improved

location

manage

SPANISH COGNATES

destino

localización

Research Companion, pages 128–137

Teach Academic Vocabulary Write the chart below on the board. Say each word aloud and have students repeat it. For Spanish speakers, point out the cognates.

Word	Part of Speech	Definition
location	noun	a place
destination	noun	the place someone is going
improved	adjective	better than before
manage	verb	control or organize someone or something

Ask: *Do you ever travel to a town or city far away? What was the <u>location</u> of the last place you traveled to?* Explain that the *location* of the place they traveled to was their *destination*. Point out that *improved* tools are better tools. Say: *The verb to improve means "to get better." Improved tools help people <u>manage</u> their jobs. They make work faster and easier.*

Build Meaning Offer language support for the following phrases:

general store = a store that sells all types of things

lack of rainfall = no rain

long-distance travel = traveling far

Unlock the Primary Source Point out the word *multitude* and explain that it means "many, many people." Explain that Ford meant that many people would be able to buy the cars his company built.

Communities Develop and Grow

Unpack the Text Write the following sentence on the board and read it aloud:

> Farmers bought goods in town, and they sold their fruits and vegetables there.

Say: *Let's look closely at the sentence so we can understand the meaning.* Remind students about compound sentences. Say: *A compound sentence is two sentences connected by a small word such as* and, but, *or* or. *This sentence uses* and. Circle the word *and.* Say: And *is a connector. Let's look at how* and *connects two sentences.* Read the first sentence:

> Farmers bought goods in town.

Say: *In this sentence, the subject is* farmers. *The verb is* bought. Point to *and.* Read the last part of the sentence, *they sold their fruits and vegetables there.* Ask students to identify the subject (*they*, which means *farmers*) and verb (*sold*). Say: *So this compound sentence is made of two sentences*:

> Farmers bought goods in town. They sold their fruits and vegetables there.

PRODUCTIVE

Have students work in pairs to write a compound sentence with *and*.

Plural Nouns with -s Review plural nouns with students. Say: *A singular noun names one person, place, or thing. A plural noun names more than one person, place, or thing.* Explain that when we talk or write about more than one noun, we usually add an *-s* to the end of the word. Draw the chart below on the board. Underline the *-s* at the end of each word in the second column. Model pronouncing the final *-s*, then have students repeat the words after you.

Singular Noun	Plural Noun
wagon	wagons
road	roads
park	parks

Distribute the graphic organizer to students. Have them work in pairs to complete the Leveled Support activities. Check their work for any errors.

Inquiry Journal, pages 142–143

Report Your Findings

Demonstrate Understanding Review the **Report Your Findings** task with students.

Think About It Review key vocabulary words. Ask students to think about what causes communities to change over time.

Write About It Place students in pairs. Have students write a paragraph telling two ways that a community might be different today from what it was in the past.

EMERGING   I think one way communities in the past were similar to today is
_____. One way they were different is _____.

EXPANDING   In my opinion, communities in the past were similar because
_____. Another way is _____. They were
different because _____.

BRIDGING   My opinion is that _____.

Provide assistance with vocabulary, pronunciation, and idea formation as needed. During the writing task, monitor and offer support with vocabulary, sentence formation, spelling, and mechanics.

Foster interaction by having students of different proficiencies discuss their opinions and the supporting reasons as they answer the Lesson Question.

Talk About It Ask partners to discuss their responses. Discuss how their community is different from the way it was a century ago.

Connect to the Essential Question Ask students to think about the changes they read about and talked about in this lesson. Which change had the biggest impact on their community?

LEVELED SUPPORT

EMERGING Have students find 3–5 more plural nouns in the text and write them in the second column. Then have them write the singular forms in the first column.

EXPANDING/ BRIDGING Have students think of nouns that are spelled with a different plural ending than *-s (-es, -ies)* and write the singular and plural nouns in the chart.

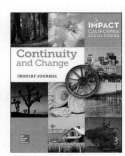

Pages 142–143

How Have People Changed the Land?

CONTENT OBJECTIVES

- Explore how people have changed the land and how these changes have affected the environment.
- Explain the difficulty of protecting the environment and meeting people's needs at the same time.
- Explain two reasons why people change the environment.

LANGUAGE OBJECTIVES

- Analyze a compound sentence.
- Analyze a sentence with two subjects.
- Recognize that the transitional word *so* expresses cause and effect.
- Understand statements of possibility with the helping verb *can*.

Pages 144–149

SPANISH COGNATE

bloquear

Inquiry Journal, pages 144–149

Introduce the Lesson

Access Prior Knowledge Before presenting the Lesson Outcomes, read the Lesson Question and find out what students already know about how people have changed the land. Ask them to tell about times they have seen the land being changed. Ask: *What are some of the changes to the land that you've seen? Why do you think people change the land? Are there any negative results from changing the land?*

 COLLABORATE Have students work in pairs to discuss how the land is changed when new streets are made in a community. Have them share their ideas with the group.

Teach Content Vocabulary Write the chart on the board. Say each word aloud and have students repeat it. For Spanish speakers, point out the cognate.

Word	Part of Speech	Definition
environment	noun	the air, land, and water where people, animals, and plants live
faucet	noun	an opening at the end of a pipe that you turn on so water comes out
reservoir	noun	a place where water is stored before it goes to people's houses
blocked	adjective	closed so that nothing can get through

Tell students that he *environment* is all around us—the land, air, and water. Water in our home usually comes from a *faucet* at a sink. The water may have traveled a long way to your faucet through pipes from a *reservoir*. Unless the pipes get *blocked*, the water flows every time. Ask questions to check understanding: *How many faucets do you have in your house? Do they ever get blocked?*

 COLLABORATE Have students work in pairs to write sentences using the words. Challenge students to use more than one word in a sentence.

Analyze the Source

Teach Academic Vocabulary Write the chart below on the board. Say each word aloud and have students repeat it. For Spanish speakers, point out the cognates.

Word	Part of Speech	Definition
several	determiner	some, but not a lot
area	noun	part of a place that is used for a particular purpose
difficulty	noun	something that makes a situation hard to deal with
entire	adjective	whole; complete

Explain to students that *several* is a determiner. Determiners, such as *all*, *few*, and *many*, tell how little or how much there is of something. *Several* means "more than one, but less than a lot." For example, *She speaks several languages: English, Spanish, and French.*

Point out that we use the word *area* to talk about a part, or section, of a place. For example, *The rain caused flooding in one __area__ of the city.* Have students share why they think we might have *difficulty* protecting the environment. Explain that *entire* means all of something.

 COLLABORATE Have students work in pairs. Students take turns covering up the definitions and telling each other the meanings of the words.

Build Meaning Offer language support for the following phrases:

meet our needs = provide what we must have

in doing so = by doing a certain action

from place to place = going from one spot to another spot

Changing Our Landscape

Unpack the Text Write the following sentence on the board and read it aloud:

A river has been blocked, so the area below the dam becomes drier.

Explain to students that this is a compound sentence: two sentences that are connected. Say: *First, let's look for the subject of the first part of the sentence.* Elicit that the subject is *a river.* Say: *Now, look let's look at the verb* has been blocked. *This means that something (a dam) blocked the river a while ago and it's still blocked now.* Circle the word *so.* Explain that *so* is also a transitional word that signals a cause-and-effect relationship. Say: *When you see the word* so, *you know that the words that follow will be a result, or an effect.* Write the word *Cause* above the first part of the sentence. Explain that *A river has been blocked* is the cause. Ask: *What is the effect of the river being blocked?* Elicit *the area below the dam becomes drier.* Write the word *Effect* above the last part of the sentence.

Draw an arrow between *Cause* and *Effect.* Ask: *Can you see the cause-and-effect relationship in this sentence?*

PRODUCTIVE Call on volunteers to try to rephrase the sentence using the transitional word *because. (The area below the dam becomes dry because a river has been blocked.)*

ACADEMIC VOCABULARY

several

area

difficulty

entire

SPANISH COGNATE

área

dificultad

entero

LEVELED SUPPORT

EMERGING Ask students to say three ways they use water, using the sentence frame:

I use water to _____.

EXPANDING/ BRIDGING Ask students to write some sentences about the way their community's environment has changed, using the sentence frame:

In my neighborhood, _____ has changed. There was _____. Now there is _____.

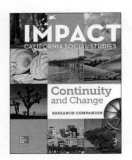

Pages 138–145

ACADEMIC VOCABULARY

benefit

major

increase

prevent

SPANISH COGNATES

beneficio

prevenir

Research Companion, pages 138–145

Teach Academic Vocabulary Write the chart below on the board. Say each word aloud and have students repeat it after you. For Spanish speakers, point out the cognates.

Word	Part of Speech	Definition
benefit	noun	a helpful effect
major	adjective	very important
increase	verb	become larger
prevent	verb	stop something from happening

Ask questions to check for understanding: *What are some underline{benefits} of living in California? What are some of the underline{major} reasons that people move here? What do you think underline{increases} the risk of forest fires? What can people do to underline{prevent} forest fires?*

Content Vocabulary Word Game: Bingo

Materials: Blank bingo cards with *Bingo* written at the top, a grid with 25 spaces, and terms and names from the lesson written at the bottom; small cards with definitions of terms or descriptions of people.

Directions: Make a list of some of the names and terms in this lesson. Give each student a blank bingo card. (Teacher Tip: Have more than 25 terms and names.) Have students fill in one term or name in random order in each space. Have a student read each definition or description. Students locate the term or name on their cards and cover it. The first student to cover five in a diagonal, horizontal, or vertical row calls out "Bingo!"

COLLABORATE Reinforce the concept of how people have changed the land. Have students work in pairs to explain how people have changed the land to meet their needs.

Build Meaning Offer language support for the following phrases:

it is pumped through sprinklers = water is pushed through metal things with holes that spray water

move water = take water from one place to another

urban sprawl = people move out of the city to the countryside

How People Use the Land

Unpack the Text Write the following sentence on the board and read it aloud:

The rocks and sand from quarries are used in cement and concrete.

Remind students that every sentence has a subject that tells who or what the sentence is about. Underline the first part of the sentence: *The rocks and sand.* Say: *There are two subjects in this sentence*: rocks *and* sand. Circle the words *are used in.* Explain that these words mean that rocks and sand are used to make cement and concrete. Another way of writing this sentence is:

Cement and concrete *are made up of* rocks and sand.

Helping Verb: *can* Check that students understand that a verb is an action word. Explain that when we talk about a possible action, something that might happen, we sometimes use the helping verb *can* before the verb. Say: *When we add the word* can, *we are saying that it's possible that an action will happen.* Write this sentence on the board: *Changing the land* can *also harm the environment.* Say: *This sentence means that if we change the land, it is possible that we will hurt the environment.* Draw the chart below on the board. Model forming and pronouncing the verb phrases, and then have students repeat the phrases after you.

GRAPHIC ORGANIZER

Verb	Verb Phrase
use	can use
flow	
get	
change	
make	
blow	

LEVELED SUPPORT

EMERGING Have students complete the second column using the helping verb *can*.

EXPANDING/ BRIDGING Have students work in pairs to make sentences with three of the verbs and *can*. Have students read their sentences aloud to each other.

 Distribute copies of the graphic organizer to students. Have students complete the Leveled Support activities.

Inquiry Journal, pages 150–151

Report Your Findings

Demonstrate Understanding Review the **Report Your Findings** task with students.

Think About It Review key vocabulary words. Ask students what causes people to change the land.

Write About It Place students in pairs. Ask them to write sentences explaining two reasons people change the land and what effects these changes have on the land.

EMERGING   I think _____ because _____.

EXPANDING   For example, _____.

BRIDGING   According to the text, _____.

During the writing task, monitor and offer support with vocabulary, sentence formation, spelling, and mechanics.

Talk About It Have partners work in small groups to discuss their responses. Ask: *What examples did your classmates give? Are the changes good or bad? Explain.*

 Foster interaction by having students of different proficiencies discuss their ideas as they answer the Lesson Question.

Connect to the Essential Question Remind students that *affected your community* means *caused your community to change.*

Pages 150–151

LESSON QUESTION

How Do Communities Develop?

CONTENT OBJECTIVES

- Explore how a community has become what it is today.
- Explain that learning about the histories of our communities helps us understand how our communities work today.
- Describe how communities develop over time.

LANGUAGE OBJECTIVES

- Recognize the meaning of the question word *how*.
- Understand the preposition *over* to describe a period of time.
- Understand sentence structure.
- Identify multiple-meaning words, such as *post, change, state, mean*.

Pages 152–157

SPANISH COGNATES

publicar

información

sitio web

blog

LEVELED SUPPORT

EMERGING Ask students to say what their favorite websites are.

EXPANDING/ BRIDGING Have students discuss something they saw recently on a website or blog, using the sentence frame:
Recently, I saw/read _____ on/in_____. It was about _____.

Inquiry Journal, pages 152–157

Introduce the Lesson

Access Prior Knowledge Before presenting the Lesson Outcomes, read the Lesson Question and find out what students already know about how their community developed. Ask: *What changes have you seen in our community?* Encourage students to talk about stores that have opened or closed, new houses that have been built, and so on. Say: *As the needs of the people change, the community also changes.*

COLLABORATE Have students work in pairs to explain two or three ways their community has changed and developed. Have them share their ideas with the group.

Teach Content Vocabulary Write the chart below on the board. Say each word aloud and have students repeat it. For Spanish speakers, point out the cognates.

Word	Part of Speech	Definition
publish	verb	arrange for a book, newspaper, magazine or other reading material to be written and sold
information	noun	facts about people, places, things, or events
website	noun	a place on the Internet where you can find information
blog	noun	a page on the internet where you write your thoughts and ideas

Say: The word <u>publish</u> *is a verb. When* <u>information</u> *is put on a* <u>website</u> *or printed in a book, magazine, or a newspaper, we say it is* published. *Say: Many people publish their thoughts on* <u>blogs</u> *and other* websites. *Point out that* blog *is a word that combines two other words. Say: The word* blog *comes from the words* web *and* log. *The word* web *is short for the World Wide Web; this is why many websites on the Internet begin with www. A* log *is a document where you can write about your thoughts and experiences. So, a blog is a website where people can record their thoughts and ideas.* Ask students what information they might find on a *blog*.

COLLABORATE Have students work in pairs to do the Leveled Support activities.

Analyze the Source

Teach Academic Vocabulary Write the chart below on the board. Say each word aloud and have students repeat it. For Spanish speakers, point out the cognates.

Ask questions to check understanding: *What are some ways that people update their friends and family about what they've been doing? What are some good things about your community that probably attract newcomers?* Say: *You can read an article in a magazine.* Ask: *Where are some other places that you can read articles?* Say: *The United States has a national anthem, or song. Do you know its name?*

COLLABORATE Erase the definitions and have students work in pairs to try to say the meaning of each word.

Build Meaning Offer language support for the following phrases:

local news = news that happens near where you live

television news = news reports on TV from all around the country

once a week = to do something just one time during a week

PRODUCTIVE Have students try to use one of the phrases in a sentence.

Explore Summarizing

Unpack the Text Write the following sentence on the board and read it aloud:

How do you tell a friend about a local event that you read or heard about?

Ask: *What kind of sentence is this?* Circle the question mark. Remind students that a question mark shows that this is a question. Say: *There's another way to tell that this sentence is a question.* Underline the word *How*. Say: How *is a question word. We use* how *plus* do you *to ask about the way something is done. We can use* how *to explain a process.* Ask: *What process is this question asking about?* Elicit that the question is asking about the way you tell a friend about things that are happening in your community.

Underline *read or heard about*. Point out the connecting word *or* between the two verbs. Remind students that or means there's a choice:

You read about a local event. OR
You heard about a local event.

ACADEMIC VOCABULARY

update

attract

article

national

SPANISH COGNATES

artículo

nacional

Pages 146–153

ACADEMIC VOCABULARY

thousands

official

role

solar

SPANISH COGNATES

oficial

solar

Research Companion, pages 146–153

Teach Academic Vocabulary Write the chart below on the board. Say each word aloud and have students repeat it after you.

Word	Part of Speech	Definition
thousands	noun	two thousand or more
official	adjective	agreed to by people who are in authority
role	noun	a person or thing's function or position
solar	adjective	relating to the sun

Ask questions to check for understanding: *There are thousands of stars in the sky. What else are there thousands of?* Say: *Official can be an adjective. It can also be a noun. For example, a government official is a person who works for the government.* Say: *Landmarks are places that had an important role in history. Can you think of any landmarks in California? Have you ever seen solar panels on a house? What do you think they do?*

Build Meaning Offer language support for the following phrases:

> **got rich** = made a lot of money

> **local neighborhood groups** = people who live in the same community who organize activities to help their neighborhood

Vocabulary Word Game: "Hot Potato" Vocabulary Elimination Game

Materials: Cards with words or phrases from this lesson
Directions: Students sit in a circle with a timer set for 3 to 5 minutes. Shuffle the cards and give the deck to a student, who draws a card. The student gives clues about the word or phrase, without saying any parts of it, trying to get other students to guess. When a student guesses correctly, the student with the deck passes it to the student next to him or her. Then that student draws a card and the game continues. The student holding the stack of cards when the timer goes off leaves the circle. Set the timer again and continue until only one student remains.

Businesses in Santa Clara

Unpack the Text Write the following sentence on the board and read it aloud:

> Over the next one hundred years, the town grew.

Point to the first part of the sentence and circle the word *Over*. Explain that *over* is a preposition that usually tells us that something is above something else. Draw a timeline on the board and write *1852* on one end and *1952* on the other. Explain that *Over the next hundred years* refers to this period of time. Ask: *What happened over this period of time? Let's keep reading.* Box *the town grew*. Say: *This sentence tells about a town that grew over a period of a hundred years. If I look at the sentence that comes before it, I can find out which town: Santa Clara.*

Unlock the Primary Source Have students look at the historic photo of Santa Clara. Explain that old photographs help us see what changes have taken place in a community. Say: *We can see how things used to look and the way they developed over time. This helps us compare the past to the present.*

Multiple-Meaning Words Draw the graphic organizer on the board. Discuss each meaning of the word *post*. Explain that when *post* is a verb, it means *to put up a sign or notice to share information*, as in "I'll *post* the notice about the concert to the school website." *Post* can also be a noun, meaning a pole in the ground. It can also mean the same as *mail* (letters and packages, etc.)

Word	Meaning #1	Meaning #2
post	put up a sign or notice to share information	a pole stuck in the ground

 COLLABORATE Write some other multiple-meaning words from the text on the board: *change* (n., v.), *state* (n., v.), *mean* (adj., v.), *mission* (n. x 2), *plant* (n. x 2, v.), *preserve* (n., v.). Distribute the graphic organizer to students and have them complete the Leveled Support activities.

Inquiry Journal, pages 158–159

Report Your Findings

Demonstrate Understanding Review the **Report Your Findings** task with students.

Think About It Review key vocabulary words. Ask students what they would like to find out about their community based on what they learned about Santa Clara.

Write About It Ask students to create a list of features about their community that they want to research further. Ask how they would use this information to encourage someone to move to their community.

Provide assistance with vocabulary, pronunciation, and idea formation as needed. During the writing task, monitor and offer support with vocabulary, sentence formation, spelling, and mechanics.

EMERGING
One feature on my list is _____. I chose it because _____.

EXPANDING/BRIDGING
I would like to research _____. I think it will encourage people to move to my community because _____.

 COLLABORATE Foster interaction by having students of different proficiencies discuss their opinions and the supporting reasons as they answer the Lesson Question.

Talk About It Place students in pairs. Ask partners to compare their lists. Have them pick features from both lists that would encourage people to move to their community.

Connect to the Essential Question Ask students to think about ways their community has changed over the years and how these changes have affected the lives of people living today.

LEVELED SUPPORT

EMERGING Have students work in pairs to write two sentences with *post* as a verb and as a noun.

EXPANDING/ BRIDGING Have students work in pairs to locate the words you wrote on the board in the text, write them in the graphic organizer, and identify the parts of speech. Challenge students to write sentences using some of the words.

 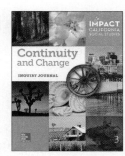

Pages 158–159

What Makes My Community Special?

CONTENT OBJECTIVES

- Explore how communities are special.
- Explain why a community is special, and how the geography, history, and cultures affect the people who live in a community.
- Explain why communities are special and how cultures of a community make it special.

LANGUAGE OBJECTIVES

- Analyze a complex sentence.
- Understand compound words.
- Learn how the names of languages are formed by adding special endings.
- Understand and form future tense verbs and sentences with *will*.

Pages 160–165

SPANISH COGNATE

pavimentar

LEVELED SUPPORT

EMERGING Ask students if they have ever felt an earthquake. How did they feel?

EXPANDING/ BRIDGING Have students work in pairs to write sentences with the words. Then have them share their sentences with the group.

Inquiry Journal, pages 160–165

Introduce the Lesson

Access Prior Knowledge Before presenting the Lesson Outcomes, read the Lesson Question and find out what students already know about what makes their community special. First, check that they understand the word *special*. Say: *If something is* special, *it's important to us. Special people, places, and things make us happy.* Ask: *What do you think is one thing that makes our community special?* Accept suggestions of places, people, and events that are part of the fabric of your community. Ask: *How does geography, history, and culture make our community a special place to live?* Explain that a community's culture gives it a special feeling or flavor. The culture of a community can be described by the people who live there, how they celebrate holidays, and how they live.

COLLABORATE Have students work in pair to explain two or three ways their community is special. Then have them share their ideas with the group.

Teach Content Vocabulary Write the chart below on the board. each word aloud and have students repeat it. For Spanish speakers, point out the cognate.

Word	Part of Speech	Definition
heritage	noun	a culture's important traditions, buildings and languages that it has had for many years
earthquake	noun	a sudden movement of the Earth's surface
pave	verb	cover a surface with stones, bricks, or tar
resort	noun	a place where many people go for a vacation

Say: *Holidays are an important part of a culture's* heritage. *What are some holidays that are important to your heritage?* Point out that the word *earthquake* is a compound word made from two words: *earth* and *quake*. Explain that an *earthquake* is when the ground shakes or moves suddenly, and that California has a lot of earthquakes. Ask: *Why do you think it's important to* pave *roads? What happens to roads that aren't paved? Can you name any* resorts *near where you live? What is it like?*

COLLABORATE Have students work in pairs to write sentences using the words.

Analyze the Source

Teach Academic Vocabulary Write the chart below on the board. Say each word aloud and have students repeat it. For Spanish speakers, point out the cognates.

ACADEMIC VOCABULARY

topic

link

conclusion

notes

SPANISH COGNATES

conclusión

nota

Word	Part of Speech	Definition
topic	noun	a subject that you talk or write about
link	noun	a connection
conclusion	noun	something you decide after thinking about all the facts and information
notes	noun	short phrases or words you write down to help you remember information

Say: *When we talk about something, we're talking about a certain* topic, *or subject. When we talk about topics, it's important to* link *our ideas together. That way, when we finish talking, our listener can make a* conclusion *about the ideas we've expressed.* Ask: *What details will you write in your* notes *about a topic you find interesting?*

Build Meaning Offer language support for these terms in the text:

horse-drawn = pulled by a horse

old fashioned = the way things were long ago

cable cars = trolleys that are used for public transportation

Linking to the Past

Unpack the Text Write the following sentence on the board and read it aloud:

The cable helps control the car when it goes downhill.

Explain to students that this is a complex sentence. It has an independent clause (underline *The cable helps control the car*) and a dependent clause (underline *when it goes downhill*). Say: *This sentence explains how the cables, or metal ropes, control the cable cars that travel up and down the streets. The first part of the sentence tells what the cable does.*

Underline *when.* Say: *The word* when *tells us there is a certain* time *that the cable does its job.* Point out that *when* connects two ideas: 1. the job the cable does, and 2. the time the cable does its job. Ask: *When does the cable help control the car?* Elicit *when it goes downhill.* Ask: *Why do you think the cable needs to control the car?* Elicit that San Francisco is hilly, so the cable helps keeps the cable car from going too fast. It helps keep people safe.

Circle *downhill.* Say: *Here is another example of a compound word. What are the two words that are linked together?* Elicit *down* and *hill.* Point out that the opposite of *downhill* is *uphill.* Use gestures to help students understand the two words.

Pages 154–161

ACADEMIC VOCABULARY

custom

language

style

honor

SPANISH COGNATES

costumbre

estilo

honrar

Research Companion, pages 154–161

Teach Academic Vocabulary Write the chart below on the board. Say each word aloud and have students repeat it after you.

Word	Part of Speech	Definition
custom	noun	a traditional way of doing something in a culture
language	noun	the words and grammar people use to communicate
style	noun	a way of designing buildings, clothing, hair, etc.
honor	verb	do something that shows respect for someone

Ask questions to check understanding: *Does your family have a <u>custom</u>, or traditional way of celebrating the new year? Do you speak more than one <u>language</u>? How would you describe the Spanish <u>style</u> of buildings in Santa Barbara?* Point out that <u>honor</u> can also be used as noun, meaning *respect*.

Build Meaning Provide language support for the following terms:

historic buildings = very old buildings that are important

original location = the place where something was first built

Vocabulary Word Game: Bean Bag Twister

Materials: Twister mat made out of craft paper or sheet of plastic and two bean bags
Directions: Draw six circles in two rows on the "twister mat." Write a vocabulary word on each circle. Place the "twister mat" on the ground. Select two students to play the game. Each student stands at either end of the mat. Read aloud a definition. Each student tosses the bag to land on the vocabulary word that you defined.

A Mix of Cultures

Unpack the Text Write the following sentences on the board and read them aloud:

These include Spanish, Chinese, Tagalog, Persian, Russian, Vietnamese, and many more.

Explain that this sentence follows a sentence about the many different languages spoken in California. The word *these* refers to *languages*. Circle the word *include*. Say: Include *is a word that tells that something is part of a group. In this case, the group is languages, and the names in this sentence are the names of languages.* Point to each language name and have students say it after you. Say: *Sometimes, language names come from the country where the language is spoken, such as* Spanish, Chinese, and Russian. Underline the endings *-ish, -ese,* and *-n.* Say: *When we change the name of a country to the name of a language, we add these endings.* Explain that other language names are different. Tagalog, for example, comes from the name of the people who first spoke this language, and *Persian* is based on Persia, the old name for Iran.

Unlock the Primary Source Check that students understand that Juan Felipe Herrera is explaining what *diversity* means. He is saying that we learn more when we accept other people. If we don't accept other people, we learn less.

Future Tense Verbs Check that students understand the present and future tenses. Explain that when we talk about *right now* we call it the *present*. Point out that when we talk or write something that is *going to happen*, we call that the *future*. Say: *When we talk about the future, we use the helping verb* will. Draw the chart below on the board. Write some verbs, such as, *talk, laugh*, and *jump*. Model forming and pronouncing the future tense, and then have students repeat the words after you.

Present	Future
talk	will talk
learn	will learn
celebrate	
share	
build	
develop	

COLLABORATE Distribute the graphic organizer to students. Have them work in pairs to complete the Leveled Support activities. Check their work for any errors.

Inquiry Journal, pages 166–175

Report Your Findings

Demonstrate Understanding Review the **Report Your Findings** task with students.

Think About It Review key vocabulary words. Ask students to recall what they learned about communities and why all communities are different.

Write About It Place students in pairs. Ask students to explain what makes communities special. Have them write a blog post about their community, its people, and its places.

EMERGING	I think _____. One reason is _____. Another reason is _____.
EXPANDING	In my opinion _____. One reason is _____. Another is _____.
BRIDGING	My opinion is that _____. One fact supporting my view is _____. Another is _____.

Provide assistance with vocabulary, pronunciation, and idea formation During the writing task, monitor and offer support as needed.

Talk About It Ask partners to share their blog posts to compare and contrast ideas. Have them brainstorm additional reasons that their community is special.

Connect to the Essential Question Ask partners to think about how history has played a part in making their community special. Have them explain how events and people from the past have affected their community.

Take Action

Project Wrap-Up Review the **Tips for Presenting** with students and check for understanding. Explain any unfamiliar terms and vocabulary. Provide support as needed as students complete the **Project Rubric** and **Project Reflection**.

EMERGING Have students complete the second column of the chart.

EXPANDING/ BRIDGING Have students write sentences using the future tense verbs in the second column.

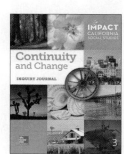

Pages 166–175

American Citizens, Symbols, and Government

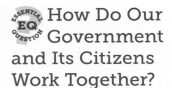

EQ How Do Our Government and Its Citizens Work Together?

Pages 176–179

SPANISH COGNATES

compromiso

(rama) ejecutiva

federal

(rama) judicial

jurado

(rama) legislativa

Inquiry Journal, pages 176–179

Introduce the Chapter

Access Prior Knowledge Read the Essential Question aloud to students. Ask: *What do you think it means to be a good citizen?* Point out that when groups of people live in a community, there must be rules and laws to protect everyone's rights. Point out that working together means that both groups—government and the citizens—share a responsibility to make things work and get along with one another. Ask how both groups can become involved in sharing the responsibility of working well together.

Research Questions Have students brainstorm in pairs "just right" research questions (neither too general nor too specific). Use examples and sentence frames to help them form questions:

"What does government do for citizens?" is **too general** because _____.	there are too many answers
"How do we describe people who follow laws?" is **too specific** because _____.	there is only one easy answer
"How can citizens and the people in the government work together to get something done?" is **just right** because _____.	there is more than one answer, but not too many answers

Inquiry Project Help students understand the project they will complete at the end of the chapter. Review any vocabulary that they don't understand, such as *constitution*, *purpose*, and *consequences*.

Word Rater Remind students that they will learn the meaning of these important words as they read through the chapter. They will make notes each time they learn something new about the word's meaning. Point out the cognates to Spanish speakers. Help them rate the words according to whether they "Know it," "Heard it," or "Don't know it."

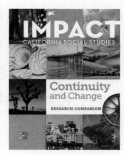

Pages 164–171

What Does It Mean to Be a Good Citizen?

Check for unfamiliar vocabulary words with students. Explain that a *democracy* is a kind of government in which the people elect, or vote for, their leaders. The leaders represent the people in government.

Write the following sentence on the board and read it aloud:

> In a democracy, your vote is your voice in government.

Circle the words *vote* and *voice*. Explain that in this sentence, the words *vote* and *voice* are compared. Say: *The verb* is *connects the words* vote *and* voice. *It tells us that these two words mean the same thing in this sentence.* Point out that *voice* is used as a metaphor for a vote. It means the leaders we vote for speak for us in government.

Connect Through Literature

Explain that *A Voice from Paris* is a fictional account of Thomas Jefferson's young daughter in Paris. It is *historical* fiction, which means it is set in the past and based on real people and events. Explain that we know Thomas Jefferson and his daughter went to Paris, but we do not know the exact words they said to each other.

Write the following sentences on the board and read it aloud:

> Patsy watched anxiously as her father read swiftly through Madison's letter. He would occasionally turn from it to refer to some part of the Constitution.

Explain that the author used her imagination when she wrote these lines. During her research, she may have discovered that Jefferson received a letter from James Madison while he was in Paris, and that he referred to the Constitution while reading the letter. However, Patsy's actions were probably not recorded, and that is where the author's imagination comes in.

Explain some difficult words and phrases in the story:

picked her way = walked carefully

diplomat = a representative of a government in another country

trade treaties = agreements about trading goods and products between countries

rudeness = behaving in a mean or impolite manner

Constitution = a plan of government

common people = ordinary people

goose quill = a feather dipped in ink to use as a pen

public opinion = what most people think

ratified = accepted

Bill of Rights = first ten amendments to the Constitution

People You Should Know

Explain some words and terms in the biographies:

Constitutional Convention = a meeting of the 13 states to write a plan of government

no running water = no faucets to bring fresh water to the houses

segregated = separated

COLLABORATE

Have students work in pairs to complete the Leveled Support activities.

LEVELED SUPPORT

EMERGING Have students identify a fact in the text.

EXPANDING Have students identify a fact and a fictional sentence in the text.

BRIDGING Have students write a factual sentence and a fictional sentence. Then have them read their sentences aloud. Ask other students to call out *fact* or *fiction*.

Why Is the Constitution of the United States Important?

CONTENT OBJECTIVES

- Explore how our government is set up.
- Examine what the Constitution is and why it is important to the people of the United States.

LANGUAGE OBJECTIVES

- Identify contrast in a sentence.
- Understand the phrase "We the people."
- Understand the prefixes *un-* and *dis-*.

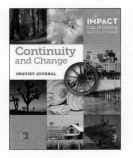

Pages 180–185

Inquiry Journal, pages 180–185

Introduce the Lesson

Access Prior Knowledge Before presenting the Lesson Outcomes, read the Lesson Question and find out what students already know about the Constitution. Ask: *What is the Constitution? What does it do for the people of the United States?* Point out that the Constitution states our beliefs. Ask if there is a similar document for your school. Give an example, such as a school mission statement. Use this comparison to lead a discussion of the importance of a document that expresses the beliefs of a group or a country.

COLLABORATE Remind students of the laws that have been generated from the Constitution. Have partners discuss why these laws are important for the people.

Teach Content Vocabulary Write the chart below on the board. Say each word aloud and have students repeat it. For Spanish speakers, point out the cognates.

SPANISH COGNATES

constitución

preámbulo

justicia

defense

Word	Part of Speech	Definition
Constitution	noun	the document that describes the structure of the U.S. government
preamble	noun	the beginning section of a document
justice	noun	the process of using laws to treat people fairly
defense	noun	protection of a country

Say: *The Constitution is an important document. One of its most important parts is the preamble. In the preamble, the authors told why they were writing it. Justice for all and the defense of our country were two of the reasons they gave.* Explain to students that in the Constitution, *defense* is spelled *defence*, which is the British spelling that people used at the time.

COLLABORATE Have students work in pairs to use the words in sentences. Have them share their sentences with the group.

Analyze the Source

Teach Academic Vocabulary Write the chart below on the board. Say each word aloud and have students repeat it. For Spanish speakers, point out the cognates.

Word	Part of Speech	Definition
union	noun	a group of states that come together to make one government
domestic	adjective	inside a particular country
promote	verb	help something happen
secure	verb	make something safe against losing it

Explain the United States was formed by the <u>union</u> of the thirteen colonies. Point out that *domestic* means inside a country. So when people talk about *domestic* problems, they mean problems in this country, not other countries. Ask: *Do you think that <u>promoting</u> world peace is a domestic responsibility?* Explain that to "<u>secure</u> the Blessings of Liberty" means that citizens' freedom will be protected.

 COLLABORATE Have students work in pairs to do the Leveled Support activities.

Build Meaning Offer language support for the following phrases:

promote the general welfare = work for the well-being of everyone

a more perfect Union = a union closer to perfect than before

 PRODUCTIVE Have students try to use one of the phrases in a sentence.

Preamble of the United States Constitution

Unpack the Text Write the following sentence on the board and read it aloud.

> The opening words show that the United States government is run by its people and for its people.

Circle *The opening words*. Ask: *What are the opening words of the Preamble?* Ellicit *We the people of the United States*. Ask: *What does this mean?* Say: *This means all of the citizens of the United States.* Point out the two phrases at the end of the sentence, *by its people and for its people.* Explain that this means the people of the United States run the government through the people they elect, and that the government works to help people.

 PRODUCTIVE Have students work in pairs to write a sentence using the phrase "We the people" to state a belief. For example:

_____ believe in freedom for all people.

We the people believe _____.

SPANISH COGNATES

unión

promover

LEVELED SUPPORT

EMERGING Have students look up *domestic* in the dictionary and find another meaning for it.

EXPANDING/BRIDGING Have students make a list of three domestic issues—that is, problems in the United States. Have them suggest a solution for each issue.

Pages 172–179

ACADEMIC VOCABULARY

convention

agreement

model

interpret

SPANISH COGNATES

convención

modelo

interpretar

Franklin, Benjamin. The Works of Benjamin Franklin Volume VI. Philadelphia: William Duane, 1809.

Research Companion, pages 172–179

Teach Academic Vocabulary Write the chart below on the board. Say each word aloud and have students repeat it. For Spanish speakers, point out the cognates.

Word	Part of Speech	Definition
convention	noun	a large meeting
agreement	noun	a decision between two people or groups to accept something
model	noun	an example for others
interpret	verb	decide what something means

Say: *In 1787. American leaders had an important meeting called the Constitutional Convention. At the meeting, they reached an agreement about how strong the U.S. government should be. Then they signed the U.S. Constitution. The Constitution describes the responsibilities of the government. Many other countries think that the Constitution works well, so they have used it as a model for their own constitutions. The United States judicial system, or courts, interpret our country's laws. They decide if the laws follow the constitution.*

COLLABORATE Reinforce the concept of why the Constitution is important to the people. Have students work in pairs to talk about the importance of the words "We the people."

How the Constitution Works

Unpack the Text Write the following sentence on the board and read it aloud.

Each branch has its own duties, but the three branches must work together.

Explain that this sentence gives us information about the three branches of government. Say: *This sentence tells us two facts about the branches of government.* Point out *each branch has its own duties.* Ask: *What does the word* duties *mean?* Elicit *jobs* or *things you are responsible for.* Say: *These ideas are connected by the transition word* but. *The word* but *shows a contrast. A contrast means one thing is different from the other thing. The contrast is that each branch has its own job to do. Yet the branches also have the job of working together. Let's write the sentence as two sentences.*

Each branch has its own duties.
The three branches must work together.

Unlock the Primary Source Read each sentence of Benjamin Franklin's quote to compare and contrast archaic and contemporary English. Ask students if they agree with his words, and to give reasons why or why not.

What Benjamin Franklin Said ...	What Benjamin Franklin's Words Mean ...
[1] Our new Consitution is now established,	[1] Our new Constitution is written and agreed to,
[2] and has an appearance that promises permanency;	[2] it looks like it will last a very long time;
[3] but in this world nothing can be said to be certain, except death and taxes.	[3] but we can never be sure of anything in life, except death and taxes.

Prefixes Check that students understand the meaning of a prefix. Say: *A prefix is letter or group of letters added to the beginning of a word*. Explain that the prefixes *un-* and *dis-* both mean "not." Draw the chart below on the board. Read the prefix in the first column. Read the root word in the second column. Model pronouncing the new word, and then have students repeat it after you. Discuss the meaning of the prefix and how it changes the meaning of a word.

Prefix	Root Word	New Word
un-	happy	unhappy
dis-	agreement	disagreement

COLLABORATE

Distribute copies of the graphic organizer to students. Have them work in pairs to complete the Leveled Support activities.

Build Meaning Provide language support for these phrases in the text:

to win their freedom = to secure independence

a set of laws = a group of rules

valuable advice = very good ideas about what to do

Inquiry Journal, pages 186–187

Report Your Findings

Demonstrate Understanding Review the **Report Your Findings** task with students.

Think About It Review key vocabulary words. Have students think about why a constitution for your classroom would be helpful.

Write About It Place students in pairs. Have them make a list of items that might be helpful for a classroom constitution.

EMERGING   From the text, I know that a constitution tells _____.

A class constitution should include _____.

EXPANDING   According to the text, a constitution should say _____.

An important point is _____.

BRIDGING   Evidence from the text shows that a constitution would benefit our classroom by _____.

The most important ideas are: _____.

Provide assistance with vocabulary, pronunciation, and idea formation as needed. During the writing task, monitor and offer support with vocabulary, spelling, and mechanics.

Talk About It Have students work together to compare and contrast their ideas, and then decide on the most important ideas to include in a class constitution. Remind them that our Constitution has a system of making laws and sharing power.

Connect to the Essential Question Have students think of ways that the Constitution helps our government and its citizens to work together.

GRAPHIC ORGANIZER

LEVELED SUPPORT

EMERGING Have students skim the text and find three words with prefixes. Have them write the root words and the new words in the chart.

EXPANDING Have students think of another word with the prefix *un-* and another with the prefix *dis-*. Have them write a sentence with each word.

BRIDGING Have partners find three things they disagree about, and write a sentence about each one.

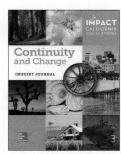

Pages 186–187

How Do the Branches of Government Work Together?

CONTENT OBJECTIVES

- Explore the branches of government.
- Examine how each branch of government works.
- Explain what each branch does and how the branches work together.

LANGUAGE OBJECTIVES

- Explore the use of repetition, fragments, and ellipses in a speech.
- Understand prepositional phrases.
- Identify the different types of sentences.

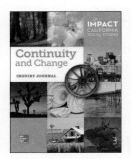

Pages 188–193

Inquiry Journal, pages 188–193

Introduce the Lesson

Access Prior Knowledge Before presenting the Lesson Outcomes, read the Lesson Question and find out what students already know about how the branches of government work together. Ask: *What happens in school when there is a problem?* Point out there are some school problems that affect everyone in the school. Ask how teachers and students work together to solve those problems. Give an example, such as trash on the playground. Use this comparison to lead a discussion of what problems the branches of government would work together to solve.

COLLABORATE
Remind students of school rules. Have partners discuss how everyone can come together to solve a group problem.

Teach Content Vocabulary Write the chart below on the board. Say each word aloud and have students repeat it. For Spanish speakers, point out the cognates.

SPANISH COGNATES

senador

representante

Word	Part of Speech	Definition
State of the Union	noun	a speech telling about how the country is doing
senator	noun	a member of the Senate
representative	noun	a member of the House of Representatives
court	noun	a place where crimes are judged

Tell students that they will learn a lot about our national government in this lesson, and how it works. Say: *You are going to learn about the president's speech, called the State of the Union. We are going to talk about senators and representatives and the work they do, and also about how important the courts are.*

COLLABORATE
Have students work in pairs to use the words in sentences. Have them share their sentences with the group.

Analyze the Source

Teach Academic Vocabulary Write the chart below on the board. Say each word aloud and have students repeat it. For Spanish speakers, point out the cognates.

Word	Part of Speech	Definition
recognize	verb	identify from earlier experience
examine	verb	look at closely and carefully
opportunity	noun	the possibility of doing something
speech	noun	a talk that someone gives to a group of people

Ask questions to check understanding: *Are you able to* _recognize_ *a song from just a few notes?* Explain that the word _examine_ means *to look closely at something*. Explain that going to school gives students the _opportunity_ to learn. Explain that a _speech_ is a talk that you give to a group.

COLLABORATE

Have students work in pairs to write sentences using two of the words. Then have them read each other's sentences aloud.

Build Meaning Offer language support for the following phrases in the text:

within our reach = possible for us to accomplish

stand up for others = support other people and their rights

in the habit = in the routine of doing something

In Their Words—Barack Obama

Unpack the Text Write the following sentences on the board and read it aloud:

> So, my fellow Americans . . . our collective future depends on your willingness to uphold your duties as a citizen. To vote. To speak out. To stand up for others, especially the weak, especially the vulnerable, . . .

Circle the ellipses. Say: *These three dots are a special punctuation mark called an* ellipsis. Explain that ellipses are used when some of the words in a sentence have been left out of the original text. Only the most important words are quoted. Underline the fragments *To vote* and *To speak out*. Ask: *Are these complete sentences?* Elicit *no, because they do not have a subject.* Say: *When we write, we usually don't use sentence fragments like this. They are not grammatically correct.* Point out that we often see fragments in printed speeches though, because speeches are designed to be heard, not read. Fragments can be a very effective way to express an idea. They are short, and they get people's attention. Also, words are often repeated in speeches so people remember them. Ask: *What words does President Obama repeat?* Elicit *To* (+ verb) ... and *especially.*

COLLABORATE

Have students work in pairs to complete the Leveled Support activities.

Unlock the Primary Source Read the excerpt from President Barack Obama's speech. Paraphrase each chunk as students follow along in the original text, matching words and phrases. Ask students for their opinion of the speech, and what they think the words mean.

ACADEMIC VOCABULARY

recognize

examine

opportunity

speech

SPANISH COGNATES

reconocer

examiner

oportunidad

LEVELED SUPPORT

EMERGING Have students list three duties that they have as students.

1. To _____

2. To _____

3. To _____

EXPANDING/BRIDGING Have students write a short speech about their duties as students, using Obama's speech as a model. Create a clozed speech on the board if students need support.

Obama, Barack. "Remarks of President Barack Obama - State of the Union Address As Delivered." State of the Union, Washington, D.C., January 13, 2016.

Pages 180–189

ACADEMIC VOCABULARY

population

limit

decide

power

SPANISH COGNATES

población

limitar

decider

poder

Research Companion, pages 180–189

Teach Academic Vocabulary Write the chart below on the board. Say each word aloud and have students repeat it. For Spanish speakers, point out the cognates.

Word	Part of Speech	Definition
population	noun	the number of people who live in a place
limit	verb	make sure something doesn't go over a certain level or amount
decide	verb	make a choice
power	noun	the ability to do something

Ask questions to check for understanding: *Can you name another state or country that has a large _population_? Why is it a good idea to _limit_ one branch's ability to control the entire government? How would you _decide_ whether something is right or wrong to do?* Say: *If we work together, we have the _power_ to make life better for everyone.*

Reinforce the concept of how branches of the government work together. Have students work in pairs to discuss what duties each branch has.

Build Meaning Provide language support for this phrase in the text:

resign, retire, or are removed = stop working because they have quit, decided to stop working because of age, or are forced from the position

Symbols and Holidays

Unpack the Text Write the following sentence on the board and read it aloud:

The leaders of our government have passed laws over the years about national and state symbols.

Say: *This sentence contains several prepositional phrases that tell us* which, what, *and* when. Remind students that prepositional phrases can tell us more about key words in a sentence. Circle *of*, *over*, and *about*. Have students say the prepositions aloud.

Explain that the information after the preposition *of* tells us *which*. Underline the phrase *The leaders of our government*. In this sentence, the word *of* points out *which* leaders. The phrase *of our government* provides more information about the leaders. Say: *The phrase* over the years *tells us when they passed the laws.* Underline *passed laws over the years*.

Then explain the prepositional phrase *about national and state symbols*. This phrase tells us *what*. Underline the phrase. Say: *Prepositional phrases give important information about a subject. They give time, location, position, and direction.*

Different Types of Sentences Review with students the different types of sentences. Say: *Sentences can make a statement, ask a question, give a command, and express an exclamation.* Draw the chart below on the board.

Read the sentences aloud, showing the differences by changing your voice.

Types of Sentences		
Statement or Command	**Exclamation**	**Question**
Each state also has its own flag.	It has the largest population of any state!	How do you feel when you see the flag?

 Distribute copies of the graphic organizer to students. Have them work in pairs to complete the Leveled Support activities.

Inquiry Journal, pages 194–195

Report Your Findings

Demonstrate Understanding Review the **Report Your Findings** task with students.

Think About It Review key vocabulary words. Have students think about how the three branches of government work together.

Write and Cite Evidence Place students in pairs. Have them write a paragraph telling which branch of government they think is the most important, citing two reasons for their choice.

EMERGING   I think _____ is the most important branch of government. My reasons are _____ and _____.

EXPANDING   In my opinion, _____. I formed this opinion because _____ and _____.

BRIDGING   My opinion is that _____ . I based my opinion on the following reasons _____ and _____.

Provide assistance with vocabulary, pronunciation, and idea formation as needed. During the writing task, monitor and offer support with vocabulary, sentence formation, spelling, and mechanics.

Talk About It Have partners take turns sharing their opinions.

 Foster interaction by having students of different proficiencies discuss their ideas as they answer the Lesson Question.

Connect to the Essential Question Have students think of ways each government branch could do a better job or working together.

GRAPHIC ORGANIZER

LEVELED SUPPORT

EMERGING Have students practice reading each of the sentences to a partner, using the correct intonation.

EXPANDING/BRIDGING Have students write a statement or command, an exclamation, and a question in their charts. Then have them practice reading each sentence with the correct intonation.

 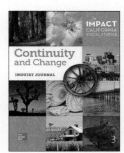

Pages 194–195

Why Do Communities Need Governments?

CONTENT OBJECTIVES

- Explore the governments in California.
- Examine why communities need government.
- Write a blog post about your local government and how it serves your community.

LANGUAGE OBJECTIVES

- Identify noun phrases (appositives).
- Understand and use possessive nouns.

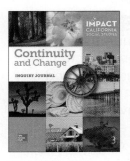

Pages 196–201

SPANISH COGNATES

juez

manager

lidér

Inquiry Journal, pages 196–201

Introduce the Lesson

Access Prior Knowledge Before presenting the Lesson Outcomes, read the Lesson Question and find out what students already know about why communities need government. Ask: *Why do we have community governments?* Compare a school community to a local community. Say: *Suppose our school was having a problem with too much noise in the halls. How could our school community solve that problem?*

COLLABORATE Have students work in pairs to discuss why schools and communities pass laws.

Teach Content Vocabulary Write the chart below on the board. Say each word aloud and have students repeat it. For Spanish speakers, point out the cognates.

Word	Part of Speech	Definition
homeland	noun	the place where a person or group of people were born
judge	noun	a person who decides about laws
manager	noun	a person who is responsible for how something works
leader	noun	a person who tells other people what to do

Point out that a _homeland_ often means an area where a group of people and their ancestors (grandparents, great-grandparents, etc.) have lived for a long, long time. Explain that a _judge_ makes decision in a court. Say: _Manager_ and _leader_ have similar meanings. When we talk about a person who works in government, we usually say leader, *not* manager.

COLLABORATE Have students work in pairs to use the words in sentences. Have them share their sentences with the group.

Analyze the Source

Teach Academic Vocabulary Write the chart below on the board. Say each word aloud and have students repeat it. For Spanish speakers, point out the cognate.

Word	Part of Speech	Definition
summarize	verb	tell something again in a shorter way
report	verb	give information about something
share	verb	show other people something that you have written or created
distinct	adjective	separate and different from something else

Explain to students that summarizing is an important skill. Say: *When we <u>summarize</u> a piece of writing, such as a <u>report</u>, we retell the main points in our own words.* Point out that before they <u>share</u> their summary, they should check that they have used their own words and made it shorter. Say: *A summary is <u>distinct</u> from the original report because it is shorter and told in different words.*

COLLABORATE Have students work in pairs to write sentences using two of the words. Then have them read each other's sentences aloud.

Build Meaning Offer language support for the following phrases:

important decision = a serious choice to make

breaking this law = disobeying a particular law

distinct from others = different and separate from others

A Supreme Court Ruling

Unpack the Text Write the following sentence on the board and read it aloud:

Samuel Worcester, a friend of the Cherokee, lived on their land.

Underline the words *a friend of the Cherokee.* Explain that this phrase comes right after the name Samuel Worcester. Explain to students that sometimes a name or other noun is followed by a group of words called a noun phrase. A noun phrase gives us more information about the name (or other noun). Ask: *What does the noun phrase tell us about Samuel Worcester?* Elicit *he was a friend of the Cherokee people.* Circle the commas either side of the noun phrase. Remind students that commas tell us to pause as we read so we can better understand the meaning of the sentence.

PRODUCTIVE Have students work in pairs to write a sentence using a noun phrase to describe a name. They can use this sentence frame:

_____, _____, _____.

    (person's name)   (noun phrase)   (what the person did)

Unlock the Primary Source Explain that Chief Justice John Marshall made a very important decision. By reading his own words, we can understand how he came to his decision. John Marshall explained that the word "nation" means that the people are distinct or separate from others.

SPANISH COGNATE

distinto

LEVELED SUPPORT

EMERGING Have students make a list of three things they sometimes share, and with whom they share the things.

EXPANDING Have students think of a TV show they watched recently, and summarize the story to their partner.

BRIDGING Have partners tell each other a story about something that happened to them recently. Then have the other partner summarize the story in writing.

Pages 190–199

ACADEMIC VOCABULARY

debate

issue

professional

design

SPANISH COGNATES

debate

diseño

profesional

Research Companion, pages 190–199

Teach Academic Vocabulary Write the chart below on the board. Say each word aloud and have students repeat it after you.

Word	Part of Speech	Definition
debate	verb	discuss
issue	verb	something that people are thinking and talking about
professional	noun	a person with a job that needs a lot of education
design	noun	draw plans to build something

Say: *When you <u>debate</u> something, it's important to think about the <u>issue</u> before you speak.* Ask: *Would you like to <u>design</u> a game?* Say: *A doctor is a <u>professional</u>. What are some other professionals?* Ask: *What are some important issues in our school or city?*

 Reinforce the concept of why communities need governments. Have students work in pairs to summarize how the legislative branch makes laws.

California State Capitol Building

Unpack the Text Write the following sentence on the board and read it aloud:

> When you visit the state capitol building, you can watch the State Assembly and Senate debate issues and vote on bills.

Explain that the sentence gives us information about visiting the state capitol. Say: *This sentence explains how you can watch the State Assembly and Senate in action. The first group of words says:* When you visit the state capitol building. Say: *The word* when *lets us know that at the time you are in this place, something will happen. Let's break the sentence into three shorter sentences:*

> You visit the state capitol building.

> You can watch the State Assembly and Senate.

> They will debate issues and vote on bills.

 Have students work in pairs to write a sentence using *When* to explain something. They can use this sentence frame:

> When you _____, _____.

Possessives Review the possessive form with students. Say: *When we talk about something that belongs to someone (or something), we use an apostrophe and the letter s.* Write the following sentence on the board and read it aloud:

We have been reading about California's government.

Circle the apostrophe and *s* in *California's*. Ask students what they mean. Elicit that they show that the government belongs to California. Explain that *California's* is a possessive.

Possessive	Noun	Phrase
California's	government	California's government
building's	history	building's history
learner's	permit	learner's permit
state's	soldiers	state's soldiers
council's	plan	council's plan

 Distribute copies of the graphic organizer to students. Have students work in pairs to complete the Leveled Support activities.

Build Meaning Provide language support for the following phrases:

longest-serving = working at a place longer than anyone else

use tax money wisely = spend money from the people carefully

share information = tell people facts that you have learned

Inquiry Journal, pages 202–203

Report Your Findings

Demonstrate Understanding Review the **Report Your Findings** task with students.

Think About It Review key vocabulary words. Have students think about how local government is different from state and national government.

Write About It Place students in pairs. Have them write blog posts describing their local government and explaining how it works.

EMERGING	Local Government: How It Works!
	Our local government has _____ It gives _____.
EXPANDING/ BRIDGING	Local Government: How It Works!
	Our local government _____. It provides _____ as well as _____.

Provide assistance with vocabulary, pronunciation, and idea formation as needed. During the writing task, monitor and offer support with vocabulary, sentence formation, spelling, and mechanics.

Talk About It Have partners share their blog posts and discuss government services.

 Foster interaction by having students of different proficiencies discuss their ideas as they answer the Lesson Question.

Connect to the Essential Question Have students think about whether citizens could survive with only local government. Invite them to share their ideas.

LEVELED SUPPORT

EMERGING Have students skim the text, find five possessive phrases, and then write the possessive, the noun, and the phrase in their charts.

EXPANDING/BRIDGING Have students write three sentences with possessive phrases.

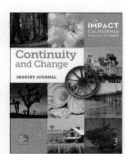

Pages 202–203

What Are Some Rules That We Must Follow?

CONTENT OBJECTIVES

- Explore the rules and laws we must follow each day.
- Examine how rules and laws keep people in our community safe.
- Write about rules you follow and tell why they are important.

LANGUAGE OBJECTIVES

- Identify words that imitate the sound they make (onomatopoeia).
- Understand cause and effect in a sentence.
- Recognize synonyms and antonyms.

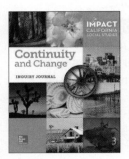

Pages 204–209

SPANISH COGNATES

accidente

equipo

programa

Inquiry Journal, pages 204–209

Introduce the Lesson

Access Prior Knowledge Before presenting the Lesson Outcomes, read the Lesson Question and find out what students already know about how rules and laws keep us safe. Ask: *What might happen in school if someone runs in the classroom?* Point out the possibilities of tripping, running into someone or something, falling down, or otherwise being injured or causing injury. Ask if classroom rules solve these problems. Compare this idea to the laws about driving in a community and ask why there are stop signs, speed limit signs, traffic lights, and so on.

COLLABORATE Remind students of playground rules. Have partners discuss how school safety affects all students. Have them discuss how community safety affects all citizens.

Teach Content Vocabulary Write the chart below on the board. Say each word aloud and have students repeat it. For Spanish speakers, point out the cognates.

Word	Part of Speech	Definition
accident	noun	something that happens that was not planned
equipment	noun	tools or gear needed for a job or game
program	noun	a series of actions or activities
consequence	noun	the result of an action

Say: *One reason we have the rule about running in the school is so we don't cause an accident.* Ask: *When you play soccer, what equipment do you need?* Say: *We are going to read about a program that helps people stay safe. If we do not follow rules, there can be consequences.*

COLLABORATE Have students work in pairs to use the words in sentences. Have them share their sentences with the group.

Analyze the Source

Teach Academic Vocabulary Write the chart below on the board. Say each word aloud and have students repeat it. For Spanish speakers, point out the cognates.

Word	Part of Speech	Definition
signal	noun	something that gives a message or warning
seriously	adverb	with importance
order	noun	the sequence in which things happen
likely	adverb	expected to happen

Say: *If we see a traffic <u>signal</u>, we know whether we should stop or go.* (Point out that the text talks about *signal words*, such as *because* and *as a result.* Explain that these words *signal*, or call out, cause-and-effect relationships in sentences.) Say: *It's important for drivers to take driving laws <u>seriously</u>. If they don't, they might have an accident.* Explain that as a noun, <u>order</u> means *something another person tells you to do.* Ask: *Is it <u>likely</u> to rain today? How do you know?*

COLLABORATE Have students work in pairs to complete the Leveled Support activities.

Safety Rules and Laws

Unpack the Text Write the following sentence on the board and read it aloud:

> The police started the *Click It or Ticket* program to protect people in cars.

First, ask students if there are any words in the sentences they don't know. Provide definitions as needed. Underline the words *Click It or Ticket.* Say: *This expression describes a community safety law.* Explain that it is a common expression in many communities. Say: *This expression is used by police officers. It means if you do not buckle your seat belt, you will get a ticket.* Explain that the word *click* imitates the sound that it makes. Say: *When we buckle our seat belt, it makes a* click *sound.* (Imitate the sound.) *That's why we say* Click It.

PRODUCTIVE Have students work in pairs to write a sentence using sound words, such as *click.* Have them think of other words, such as *buzz, splash, drip, growl, meow, chatter, moan, giggle, thump, quack, whoosh,* and *bang.* Explain their meanings as necessary. Encourage students to have fun sounding out the words.

Build Meaning Offer language support for the following phrases:

get a ticket = receive a paper from a police officer because you broke the law

pay a fine = pay money for breaking a law

must always wear a seat belt = required to fasten the safety belt in a car

PRODUCTIVE Have students try to use one of the phrases in a sentence.

ACADEMIC VOCABULARY

signal

seriously

order

likely

SPANISH COGNATES

señal

orden

LEVELED SUPPORT

EMERGING Have students give examples of a classroom rule and a rule at home by completing these sentences:

1. *At school, we have to _____.*

2. *At home, I can't _____.*

EXPANDING/BRIDGING Have students write three examples of driving laws.

Pages 200–205

ACADEMIC VOCABULARY

treat

respect

result

copy

SPANISH COGNATES

tratar

respeto

resultado

copiar

Meyers, Robert C. V. Theodore Roosevelt: Patriot and Statesman. Philadelphia, PA: P.W. Zieglar & Co., 1902.

Research Companion, pages 200–205

Teach Academic Vocabulary Write the chart below on the board. Say each word aloud and have students repeat it. For Spanish speakers, point out the cognates.

Word	Part of Speech	Definition
treat	verb	behave toward someone in a particular way
respect	verb	be kind and polite to other people
result	noun	something that happens because of something else
copy	verb	look at what someone has written, and then write the same thing

Go over the meanings, and point out that *treat, respect, result,* and *copy* can be used as both verbs and nouns. Provide examples, such as *We should treat everyone equally. / We had a treat at the party.*

Reinforce the concept of why communities need governments. Have students work in pairs to talk about the ways local governments serve the community.

Obeying Rules and Laws

Unpack the Text Write the following sentence on the board and read it aloud:

> If you know what the consequence will be, you might not break a rule.

Check that students understand the word *consequence.* Say: *In this sentence, we will look at cause and effect. A* cause *is what makes something happen. The* effect *is the thing that happens; it is the result.* Circle the word *If.* Explain that this word sets up the cause and effect in this sentence. It lets the reader know that if a certain thing happens, it is going to cause something else to happen. Ask: *What is the cause in this sentence?* Elicit *If you know what the consequence will be.* Ask: *What is the effect in this sentence?* Elicit *you might not break a rule.* Point out that the effect is the result.

Unlock the Primary Source Explain that Theodore Roosevelt was President of the United States between 1901 and 1909. Help students understand his words.

What President Roosevelt Said ...	What Roosevelt's Words Mean ...
[1] Not only should there be complete liberty in matters of religion and opinion,	[1] All people should be free to practice any religion and say anything they want,
[2] but complete liberty for each man to lead his life as he desires,	[2] and all people should be able to live as they want,
[3] provided only that in so doing he does not wrong his neighbor.	[3] as long as they don't hurt anyone else.

Say: *Roosevelt gave this speech over a hundred years ago. Is it still true today?* Discuss why these words are still important today.

Synonyms and Antonyms Explain that in English, there are many words that have a similar meaning, or mean the same thing. These words are called *synonyms*. Say: *We can use synonyms to avoid using the same word in our writing over and over again. They can add a different shade of meaning to a common word.* Explain that other words mean the opposite; these words are called *antonyms*. Write the chart below on the board. Invite students to provide other examples of words and their synonyms and antonyms.

Word	Synonym	Antonym
stop	halt	go
protect	guard	endanger

Distribute the graphic organizer to students. Have them work in pairs to complete the Leveled Support activities.

Build Meaning Provide language support for phrases in the text:

treated equally = behaved the same way toward everyone

cut in line = push into a line instead of getting at the end

without permission = do something without asking if you can

Inquiry Journal, pages 210–211

Report Your Findings

Demonstrate Understanding Review the **Report Your Findings** task with students.

Think About It Review key vocabulary words. Have students think about why it is important to have rules and laws.

Write About It Place students in pairs. Have them describe rules they follow at home and the consequences for breaking them.

EMERGING   There are two rules I follow at home. The first is _____.
If I break the rule, the consequence is _____. The second is _____. If I break the rule the consequence is _____.

EXPANDING/ BRIDGING   The two rules I follow at home are _____ and _____. The consequences for breaking the rules are _____.

Provide assistance with vocabulary, pronunciation, and idea formation as needed. During the writing task, monitor and offer support with vocabulary, sentence formation, spelling, and mechanics.

Talk About It Have partners share their rules, the consequences, and the reasons for the rules. How are they similar or different?

Foster interaction by having students of different proficiencies discuss their ideas as they answer the Lesson Question.

Connect to the Essential Question Have students discuss this question in a small group.

GRAPHIC ORGANIZER

LEVELED SUPPORT

EMERGING Have students add the words *big*, *chilly*, and *calm* to their charts, and write synonyms and antonyms for the words. They can use a dictionary if needed.

EXPANDING/BRIDGING Have students write three sentences that include antonyms. Each sentence should include the word *but*, with one of the antonyms in each clause.

Example: *I am tall, but my brother is short.*

 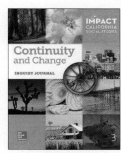

Pages 210–211

How Has Citizenship Changed Over Time?

CONTENT OBJECTIVES

- Explore what it means to be a good citizen and how citizenship has changed over time.
- Examine how people affect their community and country.
- List the ways citizenship has changed over time and what it is like to be a U.S. citizen today.

LANGUAGE OBJECTIVES

- Identify a *before* clause in a sentence.
- Understand words in a series.
- Form the plural of nouns ending in *-y*.

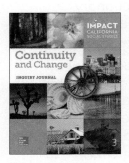

Pages 212–217

SPANISH COGNATE

involucrado

Inquiry Journal, pages 212–217

Introduce the Lesson

Access Prior Knowledge Before presenting the Lesson Outcomes, read the Lesson Question and review what students already know about being a citizen. Ask: *Do you think all American citizens have always been treated equally?* Point out that women and people of color have not always had all the rights of citizens. Explain that people fought hard to change unfair laws. Now there is equality for all citizens. They have the same rights.

 Have students review the concept of people being treated equally and fairly. Have them discuss some ways that people may not have been treated fairly in the past.

Teach Content Vocabulary Write the chart below on the board. Say each word aloud and have students repeat it. For Spanish speakers, point out the cognate.

Word	Part of Speech	Definition
citizenship	noun	the condition of being a citizen
duty	noun	something you have to do
involved	adjective	taking part (participating) in an activity
oath	noun	a promise

Ask questions to check comprehension: *What kinds of actions show good <u>citizenship</u>?* Elicit helping others and obeying laws. Ask: *Does a citizen have a <u>duty</u> to obey laws? What can we do to get <u>involved</u> in our local government?* Elicit that we can stay informed and know what's going on in our neighborhood and community. Ask: *Why do you think new citizens have to take an <u>oath</u> to support the Constitution and the laws of the United States? Is this a good idea? Why or why not?*

 Have students work in pairs to use the words in sentences. Have them share their sentences with the group.

Analyze the Source

Teach Academic Vocabulary Write the chart below on the board. Say each word aloud and have students repeat it. For Spanish speakers, point out the cognates.

Word	Part of Speech	Definition
cause	noun	a goal you believe in
change	verb	make different
compare	verb	study to discover how something is alike or different
paragraph	noun	a group of sentences about a certain topic

Tell students that important people like Susan B. Anthony and Martin Luther King, Jr. fought for _causes_ they felt strongly about. Their work helped our nation _change_ for the better. Explain that when we _compare_ two things, we look at the ways they are alike and different. Say: _In a paragraph, all of the sentences should be about the same topic or idea._

COLLABORATE Have students work in pairs to write sentences using two of the words. Then have them read each other's sentences aloud.

Build Meaning Offer language support for the following phrases in the text:

joined together = connected as a team

constitutional right = a right guaranteed by the Constitution

guarantees voting rights = makes sure everyone is able to vote

PRODUCTIVE Have students try to use one of the phrases in a sentence.

Women Fight for Equality

Unpack the Text Write the following sentence on the board and read it aloud.

> She was even arrested when she voted in an election before women had the right to vote.

Explain to students that this sentence gives us information about Susan B. Anthony. Say: _Let's break the sentence up into chunks._ Underline the phrase: _She was even arrested._ Point out that this phrase explains what happened to Susan B. Anthony. Circle the two transition words, _when_ and _before._ Explain that the words that follow these transition words add details to the first part of the sentence. Underline the phrase: _when she voted in an election._ These words explain what Susan B. Anthony did. Underline the phrase: _before women had the right to vote._ Say: _These words explain why she was arrested._ Explain that the word _before_ lets us know that there was a time when women did not have the right to vote. The two ideas in the sentence are connected. Say: _Let's write the sentence as two sentences:_

> Long ago, women did not have the right to vote.

> Susan B. Anthony was arrested when she voted in an election.

PRODUCTIVE Have students work in pairs to do the Leveled Support activities.

SPANISH COGNATES

causa

comparer

parráfo

LEVELED SUPPORT

EMERGING Have students complete these sentences.

1. Yesterday, I _____ before I had breakfast.

2. I usually _____ before I go to bed.

3. Students should _____ before they take a test.

EXPANDING/BRIDGING Have students work in pairs to write two sentences using the word _before._ Use this sentence frame:

_____ before _____.

Pages 206–215

Kennedy, John F. Inaugural Address of President John F. Kennedy. Washington D.C., January 20, 1961.

ACADEMIC VOCABULARY

steps

opinion

informed

expected

SPANISH COGNATES

opinión

informado

Research Companion, pages 206–215

Teach Academic Vocabulary Write the chart below on the board. Say each word aloud and have students repeat it. For Spanish speakers, point out the cognates.

Word	Part of Speech	Definition
steps	noun	parts of a process
opinion	noun	the way a person thinks about an issue
informed	adjective	aware of changes in the world
expected	adjective	not a surprise

Ask questions to check understanding: *When you're putting something together, do you follow the <u>steps</u> in the directions, or just figure it out as you go along? In your <u>opinion</u>, is it better to follow the directions?* Say: *If you read the directions, you're <u>informed</u> about how to put the thing together, and each step in the process will be <u>expected</u>, and not a surprise.*

COLLABORATE Reinforce the concept of how citizenship has changed over time. Have students work in pairs to talk about the problems women faced about voting.

Build Meaning Provide language support for the following phrases:

    pass a test = succeed on a test

    oath of allegiance = promise to be loyal to the country

    right to worship = the right to go to church if they choose

Being a Good Citizen

Unpack the Text Write the following sentence on the board and read it aloud:

    Taxes pay for services such as schools, libraries, and police and fire departments.

Ask: *What is the subject of this sentence?* Elicit *taxes.* Review that taxes are the money that people pay so the government can do its work. Say: *The sentence tells us that taxes pay for services that the people need.* Ask: *What is the object of this sentence? That is, what are the taxes used for?* Elicit that taxes are used to provide schools, libraries, and police and fire departments. Point out that this sentence has FOUR objects. This is called a compound object. Circle the commas, and remind students that a comma is placed between words in a series. Point out that there is no comma needed between *police* and *and* because they are both departments.

Unlock the Primary Source Review with students that John F. Kennedy was the president of the United States between 1961 and 1963. Discuss the meaning of this famous passage from his inaugural address. If possible, find a video of this speech to show students. Point out the words that are repeated. (Ask; your country). Ask students why they think President Kennedy repeated these words. What effect do they have on the listener? Remind students that leaders often repeat words in speeches so people remember them.

What President Kennedy Said ...	What Kennedy's Words Mean ...
[1] Ask not what your country can do for you	[1] Don't ask what you are going to get just for being an American.
[2] ask what you can do for your country.	[2] Instead, you should find out ways you can help make the country better.

Plural Nouns: -y to -ies Remind students that most plural nouns end with -s or -es. Explain that some singular nouns end in -y. When nouns end in a consonant + y, we change the y to an i and add -es to form a plural. Write the chart below on the board with the word *responsibility* in the first column. In the second column, write the word again, and then erase the y and add -ies. Repeat with the other words.

Singular Noun Ending in -y	Plural Noun Ending in *-ies*
responsibility	responsibilities
community	
library	
family	

COLLABORATE Distribute the graphic organizer to students. Have them work in pairs to complete the Leveled Support activities.

Inquiry Journal, pages 218–219

Report Your Findings

Demonstrate Understanding Review the **Report Your Findings** task with students.

Think About It Review key vocabulary words. Have students think about how citizenship has changed over the years in this country.

Write About It Place students in pairs. Have them complete the Venn diagram.

EMERGING   I understand that long ago _____. Today
_____.

EXPANDING   According to the text, in the past _____. Because of
_____, now _____.

BRIDGING   From the text evidence I learned that in the past _____.
However, today _____.

Provide assistance with vocabulary, pronunciation, and idea formation as needed. During the writing task, monitor and offer support with vocabulary, sentence formation, spelling, and mechanics.

Talk About It Have partners compare their diagrams and discuss similarities and differences.

COLLABORATE Foster interaction by having students of different proficiencies discuss their ideas as they answer the Lesson Question.

Connect to the Essential Question Have students think of ways being a good citizen benefits their community as well as the United States.

EMERGING Have students write the singular and plural forms of these verbs in their charts: *country, story, baby.*

EXPANDING Have students think of three more nouns that end in -y, and write the singular and plural forms of the nouns in their charts.

EMERGING Have students write two sentences, each including the plural form of one of the nouns in the chart.

Pages 218–219

How Have Heroes Helped Their Communities?

CONTENT OBJECTIVES

- Explore real people who make their communities and nation better.
- Examine how people have solved problems.
- Relate stories of real Americans who helped solve problems in their communities.

LANGUAGE OBJECTIVES

- Understand sentence structure.
- Recognize proper nouns.

Pages 220–225

SPANISH COGNATES

conciencia

proclomación

ilegal

Inquiry Journal, pages 220–225

Introduce the Lesson

Access Prior Knowledge Before presenting the Lesson Outcomes, read the Lesson Question and find out what students already know about community heroes. Ask: *What is a hero?* Point out that when people do heroic acts, there is often a story about them in the newspaper or on television. Ask: *Why do you think people like to read or hear stories about heroes?* Ask students to give some examples of heroic acts.

COLLABORATE Explain that everyone is capable of heroic acts. Have students make a list of people they consider heroes. Have them share their list with the group.

Teach Content Vocabulary Write the chart below on the board. Say each word aloud and have students repeat it. For Spanish speakers, point out the cognates.

Word	Part of Speech	Definition
conscience	noun	the part of you that tells you an action is right or wrong
trial	noun	a legal process in which a court decides if someone is guilty
proclamation	noun	an official public statement
illegal	adjective	against the law

Ask students if they ever hear a "little voice" inside when they are tempted to do something they know they shouldn't do. Explain that this "little voice" is called a _conscience_. Our conscience reminds us of the difference between right and wrong. When our conscience "speaks" to us, we can either listen to it or we can ignore it. Say: *We're going to learn about people who listened to their conscience, such as Anne Hutchinson, who went on _trial_, and Abraham Lincoln, who made a _proclamation_ that made slavery _illegal_.* Explain that this means slavery was against the law, and therefore people were freed from slavery.

COLLABORATE Have students share ideas about why people should "listen" to their conscience. Why is it important?

Analyze the Source

Teach Academic Vocabulary Write the chart below on the board. Say each word aloud and have students repeat it. For Spanish speakers, point out the cognate.

Word	Part of Speech	Definition
reread	verb	read again
solve	verb	find an answer to a problem
disagree	verb	have a different opinion than someone else

Explain that when we _reread_ a text, we start over and read it from the beginning. Note that sometimes rereading will help you _solve_ a problem because you find the answer when you reread. Say: *When two people _disagree_ about a lot of issues, they can still be friends.* Ask questions to check understanding of the information.

 COLLABORATE Have students work in pairs to write sentences using two of the words. Then have them read each other's sentences aloud.

Build Meaning Offer language support for the following phrases:

speak her mind = say what she thinks

think for herself = make her own decisions

 PRODUCTIVE Have students try to use one of the phrases in a sentence.

Anne Hutchinson: A Hero for Freedom

Unpack the Text Write the following sentence on the board and read it aloud:

> The ministers who disagreed with Anne had her arrested.

First, check that students understand all the vocabulary and clarify any words as needed. Remind them that they are exploring cause and effect in this lesson. Say: *There are some words we can use to talk about cause and effect. Two common words are* because *and* so. Explain that whenever we see these words in a sentence, we know there's a cause-and-effect relationship. Say: *Let's unpack this sentence to find the cause and the effect.* Ask: *What is the cause?* Elicit that the ministers disagreed with Anne. Ask: *What was the effect?* Elicit that Anne was arrested. Say: *We can rewrite this sentence using* so *or* because:

Cause   **Effect**
The ministers disagreed with Anne, <u>so</u> they had her arrested.

Effect   **Cause**
Anne was arrested <u>because</u> the ministers disagreed with her.

 PRODUCTIVE Have students work in pairs to do the Leveled Support activities.

ACADEMIC VOCABULARY

reread

solve

disagree

SPANISH COGNATE

resolver

LEVELED SUPPORT

EMERGING Have students connect these sentences using *so.*

The court told Anne to leave the community. She left.

EXPANDING/BRIDGING Have students complete these cause-and-effect sentences:

The court ordered Anne to leave the community, so _____.

Anne left the community because _____.

Pages 216–225

ACADEMIC VOCABULARY

refuse

positive

protest

standard

SPANISH COGNATES

positivo

protesta

Lincoln, Abraham. The Emancipation Proclamation. Washington, D.C., January 1, 1863.

Research Companion, pages 216–225

Teach Academic Vocabulary Write the chart below on the board. Say each word aloud and have students repeat it after you. For Spanish speakers, point out the cognates.

Word	Part of Speech	Definition
refuse	verb	not do something, even if other people want you to do it
positive	adjective	good
protest	noun	an action that shows you disagree with something; for example, shouting and holding signs
standard	noun	a rule or example that other things are compared to

Ask questions to check for understanding: *Do you ever _refuse_ to do something? What do you refuse to do, and why? Can you name someone who has had a _positive_ effect on you? What do you think people sometimes _protest_ about? Have you ever seen a protest?* Explain that always telling the truth is a *standard* we all should try to achieve or aim for.

 COLLABORATE Reinforce the concept of how heroes help their communities. Have students work in pairs to talk about how a hero can make a community better by their brave actions.

Build Meaning Offer language support for the following phrases in the text:

    speak against = talk against someone or something

    risked her life = was in danger of dying

    the side of a road = the edge of a street

 PRODUCTIVE Have students think of an example of someone who risks their life for another person. (Examples include firefighters and others who rescue people in danger.)

American Heroes

Unpack the Text Write the following sentence on the board and read it aloud.

> The routes she followed and the houses where people could hide were known as the Underground Railroad.

Check that students understand the word *routes*. Explain that sentences often begin with the subject. Say: *This sentence has a compound subject. That means it has two subjects. What are the subjects in this sentence?* Elicit *routes* and *houses*. Point out that the subjects in this sentence are followed by nouns and verbs. The subjects plus the nouns and verbs are called *clauses*. Underline *The routes she followed* and *the houses where people could hide*. Say: *These are* clauses.

Unlock the Primary Source Read the words from Abraham Lincoln's Emancipation Proclamation aloud, and then read the contemporary version. Have students track the print in the original text, matching words and phrases. Ask them how the words make them feel.

Archaic English	Contemporary English
"... I do order and declare that all persons held as slaves within said designated States, and parts of States, are, and henceforward shall be free; ..."	I am ordering that all slaves within the states are now free and will be free from now on.

Proper Nouns Say: *A proper noun names a particular person, place, or thing.* Draw the chart below on the board. Have students skim the Research Companion text and find a proper noun. Have them think of a common noun that could take its place in the sentence. Model pronouncing the proper noun, and then have students repeat the words after you.

Proper Noun	Common Noun
American Red Cross	organization
Civil War	war
Congress	lawmakers
Geneva Convention	agreement (treaty)

 Distribute the graphic organizer to students. Have them work in pairs to complete the Leveled Support activities.

Inquiry Journal, pages 226–227

Report Your Findings

Demonstrate Understanding Review the **Report Your Findings** task with students.

Think About It Review key vocabulary words. Have students think about problems from the past that Americans have tried to solve.

Write About It Place students in pairs. Have them choose an issue from the past and explain how people worked to solve it. Have them explain the results of their actions.

EMERGING From the text, I know one problem was _____. People did _____ to solve it. The result was _____.

EXPANDING According to the text, _____ was a big issue. People _____. The result was _____.

BRIDGING Evidence from the text shows _____. The problem was solved _____. The result was _____.

Talk About It Have partners discuss how the person or people helped make the United States a better place.

Connect to the Essential Question Have students think of ways Americans can work together to solve problems in a community.

LEVELED SUPPORT

EMERGING Have students write the proper nouns below in the chart, and then write the correct common nouns next to them.

United States
The name of your school
The name of your city or town

EXPANDING/BRIDGING Have students write the common nouns below in the chart, and then write corresponding proper noun next to them.

organization
war
leader

Pages 226–227

How Can Citizens Build Strong Communities?

CONTENT OBJECTIVES

- Explore what makes a strong community.
- Examine how people make a difference in their communities.
- Describe characteristics of good leaders. Write about how citizens can help their communities.

LANGUAGE OBJECTIVES

- Identify prepositional phrases.
- Understand verb phrases in a sentence.
- Explore adverbs.

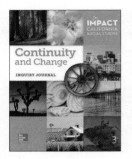

Pages 228–233

SPANISH COGNATES

servicio a la comunidad

conservación

Inquiry Journal, pages 228–233

Introduce the Lesson

Access Prior Knowledge Before presenting the Lesson Outcomes, read the Lesson Question and find out what students already know about how citizens can build strong communities. Ask: *What makes a community strong?* Point out one of the most important aspects of a strong community is citizen participation. Say: *How can citizens take part in their community to make it stronger?*

COLLABORATE Remind students of their school community. Have partners discuss how everyone can work together to make their school a strong community.

Teach Content Vocabulary Write the chart below on the board. Say each word aloud and have students repeat it. For Spanish speakers, point out the cognates.

Word	Part of Speech	Definition
volunteer	verb	do something without being paid for it, usually to help someone
community service	noun	work a person does without pay to help his or her community
conservation	noun	the process of protecting something, such as water

Ask questions to check understanding: *Have you ever <u>volunteered</u>? What did you do? What is one way that young people can do <u>community service</u>? What does water <u>conservation</u> do for everyone? Why is it important?*

COLLABORATE Have students work in pairs to use the words in sentences. Have them share their sentences with the group.

Analyze the Source

Teach Academic Vocabulary Write the chart below on the board. Say each word aloud and have students repeat it. For Spanish speakers, point out the cognates.

Word	Part of Speech	Definition
characteristic	noun	a feature that something has
graph	noun	a drawing that uses lines, dots, or bars to show change
chart	noun	a table that presents data

Point out that all the words are nouns. Say: *When we think about characters in a book, we think about their <u>characteristics</u>, such as whether they are quiet, talkative, funny, heroic, athletic, and so on. We use <u>graphs</u> and <u>charts</u> in many of our classes because they are good ways to show a lot of information in a way that's easy to understand.*

 COLLABORATE Have students work in pairs to write sentences using two of the words. Then have them read each other's sentences aloud.

Build Meaning Offer language support for the following phrases:

where we live = where our home is

share certain beliefs = believe the same things as other people

 PRODUCTIVE Have students work in pairs to do the Leveled Support activities.

Building Community

Unpack the Text Write the following sentence on the board and read it aloud:

In a strong community people try to do what is best for everybody.

Explain that prepositional phrases give important information in a sentence. Say: *This sentence contains several prepositional phrases that tell us* where *and* for whom. Circle *in* and *for.* Have students say the prepositions aloud. Point out that the first prepositional phrase is *In a strong community.* Underline the phrase. Explain that the information after the preposition *in* tells us *where.* In this sentence, the word *in* tells where (*in a community*), and *in a strong community* provides more information about the people. Point out that the second prepositional phrase is *for everybody.* Underline the words. Say: *This phrase tells us that people try to do what is best for all of the people.*

 PRODUCTIVE Have students work in pairs to write a sentence using a prepositional phrase. Use this sentence frame:

In _____, students _____.

ACADEMIC VOCABULARY

characteristic

graph

chart

SPANISH COGNATES

característica

gráfico

LEVELED SUPPORT

EMERGING Have students write a sentence about something they believe in, using this sentence frame:

I believe that _____.

EXPANDING Have students talk about their beliefs, and find two things they both believe in. Then have them write sentences using this sentence frame:

We both believe that _____.

BRIDGING Have students talk about their beliefs, and find something they disagree about. Then have them try to persuade each other to change their opinion.

Pages 226–233

ACADEMIC VOCABULARY

reduce

trust

force

solution

SPANISH COGNATES

reducer

forzar

solución

Smith, Karen. Health Leaders Invite Innovation to Improve California's Health. Sacramento, CA. September 14, 2016.

Research Companion, pages 226–233

Teach Academic Vocabulary   Write the chart below on the board. Say each word aloud and have students repeat it. For Spanish speakers, point out the cognates.

Word	Part of Speech	Definition
reduce	verb	make something less in size or number
trust	verb	believe someone is good and honest
force	verb	make someone do something against their will
solution	noun	the answer to a problem

Ask questions to check understanding: *How can we reduce the amount of paper we use? Which people do you trust the most? Why do police officers force people to obey the traffic laws? When you are looking for a solution, do you ask other people for their opinion?*

COLLABORATE Reinforce the concept of how citizens can build strong communities. Have students work in pairs to talk about community service projects they could start in their own communities.

Build Meaning   Provide language support for the following phrases:

     a way of life = how someone lives

     live in the same area = live in the same part of the land

     collects trash = picks up trash and throws it away

Ways to Make a Difference

Unpack the Text   Write the following sentence on the board and read it aloud:

     There are groups that build houses for people, run food pantries, and collect used clothing.

Check that students understand the meaning of the term *food pantries*. Explain that this sentence contains a series of verb phrases. Explain that verb phrases are verbs and other words that together form an action. Point out that the verb phrases in this sentence provide important details. They explain the types of actions people can perform to help others. Circle the verbs *build, run*, and *collect*. Have students identify the nouns that follow each of these verbs. Ask: *What are the verb phrases in this sentence?* Elicit *build houses*, *run food pantries*, and *collect used clothing*.

Unlock the Primary Source   Read the quote from Dr. Karen Smith in the first column. Then read the easier sentence structure in the 2nd column. Ask students if they agree with Dr. Smith's words. Have them explain why.

What Karen Smith Said ...	What Karen Smith's Words Mean ...
[1] "Health begins in our homes, schools, workplaces, neighborhoods, and communities.	[1] People learn about health at home, school, at work, in their neighborhoods, and in their communities.
[2] To have healthy people and healthy communities, we have to create the social and physical environments that give every Californian the opportunities we need to be healthy."	[2] We have to make it easy for people to get what they need to be healthy.

Adverbs Remind students that we can give more information about a verb by using an adverb. An adverb often ends in *-ly*. In the Research Companion, point out the adverbs *clearly* and *directly*, which are used to modify *explain* and *talk*. Draw the chart on the board. Model the formation of adverbs by writing adjectives in the chart and inviting students to tell you what the adjective would be. Challenge them to use their new adverb in a sentence. If a student suggests a word such as *bigly*, explain that not all adjectives make good adverbs.

Adjective + *-ly*	Adverb
slow + *ly*	slowly
sharp + *ly*	sharply
sad + *ly*	sadly

 Distribute the graphic organizer to students. Have them work in pairs to complete the Leveled Support activities.

Inquiry Journal, pages 234–237

Report Your Findings

Demonstrate Understanding Review the **Report Your Findings** task with students.

Think About It Review key vocabulary words. Have students think about a problem that affects their community right now.

Write About It Place students in pairs. Have them write a paragraph describing the problem and how they would solve it.

EMERGING   I think _____ is a big problem. I can help solve it by _____.

EXPANDING   In my opinion, _____ is a big problem. I can _____ to solve it.

BRIDGING   My opinion is that _____. I would solve _____.

Provide assistance with vocabulary, pronunciation, and idea formation as needed. During the writing task, monitor and offer support with vocabulary, sentence formation, spelling, and mechanics.

Talk About It Have partners compare problems and solutions. Have them offer different solutions to their partner's problem.

 Foster interaction by having students of different proficiencies discuss their ideas as they answer the Lesson Question.

Connect to the Essential Question Have students think of ways people in the community can work together to make their community a better place.

Take Action

Project Wrap-Up Review the **Tips for Presenting** with students and check for understanding. Explain any unfamiliar terms and vocabulary. Provide support as needed as students complete the **Project Rubric** and **Project Reflection**.

LEVELED SUPPORT

EMERGING Have students add three adjectives to their chart, and write the adverbs next to the adjectives. Possible adjectives: *quick, loud, quiet.*

EXPANDING Have students write a sentence using each adverb in the chart.

BRIDGING Have students think of three more adverbs that end in *-ly*, and write a sentence with each adverb.

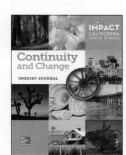

Pages 234–237

Economics of the Local Region

 How Do People in a Community Meet Their Needs?

Pages 238–241

SPANISH COGNATES

beneficio

(recursos de) capital

economía

exportar

capital humano

recursos humanos

importar

manufacturar

Inquiry Journal, pages 238–241

Introduce the Chapter

Access Prior Knowledge Read the Essential Question aloud to students. Ask: *What are needs?* Review with students that *needs* are the things we need in order to exist or survive. If our needs aren't met, we can't stay alive. Compare needs and wants. Explain that *wants* are the things we would like to have, that make life fun, but we don't need them in order to exist. Ask: *What are some wants that people have?* Tell students they will learn a lot about needs and wants in this chapter.

Explain to students that resources are the things we use. Businesses also use resources to make their goods (products) and transport (drive) them to our communities. Farmers use resources, too. Point out that some resources are natural, such as vegetables, livestock (farm animals), fruit, seafood (fish), and lumber (wood). The sun, wind, and water are also resources. Tell students they will also learn a lot about money in this chapter.

Research Questions Have students brainstorm in pairs "just right" research questions (neither too general nor too specific). Use examples and sentence frames to help them form questions:

"What resources do businesses in California use?" is **too general** because _____.	there are too many answers
"How do restaurants make money?" is **too specific** because _____.	there is only one easy answer
"How do businesses in a community help meet people's needs?" is just right because _____.	there is more than one answer, but not too many answers

Inquiry Project Help students understand the project they will complete at the end of the chapter. Review any vocabulary that they don't understand, such as *blog, local, select,* and *conduct.*

Word Rater Remind students that they will learn the meaning of these important words as they read through the chapter. They will make notes each time they learn something new about the word's meaning. Point out the cognates to Spanish speakers. Help them rate the words according to whether they "Know it," "Heard it," or "Don't know it."

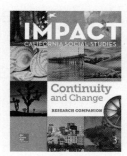

Pages 236–239

How Do People Meet Their Needs?

Check any unfamiliar vocabulary words and clarify for students. Explain that a *trade-off* is a compromise, or a situation that involves giving up something in order to gain another. Give an example: A community is building a swimming pool in the local park. People are happy to have a pool, but sad to lose part of the park.

Write the following sentence on the board and read it aloud:

> Sometimes, saving money rather than spending it is how people can best meet their needs.

Circle the words *saving* and *spending*. Explain that these words are antonyms—they have the opposite meaning, like *hot* and *cold*. Underline the words *rather than*. Say: *The words* rather than *show a contrast or a choice. You can do one of two things: You can either* spend *your money or you can* save *your money.*

Connect Through Literature

Explain that the story *Clothes with an IQ* is an article. An article is a piece of writing that we often find in newspapers, magazines, or online. This article describes new types of fabrics that people have designed for a special purpose.

Write the following sentence on the board and read it aloud:

> If a smidge of space debris punctures the suit, the gel oozes into the hole to seal it up.

Circle the word *smidge*. Tell students that writers try to use interesting or unusual words rather than the same words over and over again. Explain that writers use these words to make their articles more enjoyable to read. Ask: *What word could the author have used instead of the word* smidge? Elicit *a little bit*. Point out synonyms for other words in the sentence: *debris/junk* or *trash; punctures/cuts; oozes/drips; seal up/close.*

Explain these words and phrases in the article:

electronic components = parts that are computer-related

blood pressure = the pressure of the blood in the body

alert you = tell or warn you

space capsule = a vehicle that carries astronauts into space

ski slope = a hill covered in snow

solar panel = a piece of equipment that changes sunlight into electricity

all about speed = speed is very important

skintight = fitting very close against the skin

hardens on impact = becomes hard when it touches something

COLLABORATE Have students work in pairs to complete the Leveled Support activities.

LEVELED SUPPORT

EMERGING Have students write the antonyms for following words: *outside (inside); tiny (huge); new (old); day (night); buy (sell); remember (forget); import (export);*

EXPANDING/BRIDGING Have students choose one of the pairs of antonyms above and use them in sentences.

How Do Businesses Use Resources?

CONTENT OBJECTIVES

- Examine what kinds of resources businesses use.
- Understand how businesses in California provide goods and services.
- Describe how businesses in California use resources.

LANGUAGE OBJECTIVES

- Identify transition word *because*.
- Understand adjective clauses.
- Use an apostrophe to show ownership.

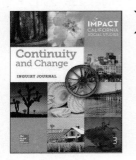

Pages 242–247

SPANISH COGNATES

agricultura

clima

Inquiry Journal, pages 242–247

Introduce the Lesson

Access Prior Knowledge Before presenting the Lesson Outcomes, read the Lesson Question and find out what students already know about the kinds of resources businesses use. Explain that *resources* are things we use to create products and services. Ask: *What are some resources that businesses in California use?* Elicit answers such as *fruit*, *vegetables*, *seafood*, and *lumber*.

Teach Content Vocabulary Write the chart below on the board. Say each word aloud and have students repeat it. For Spanish speakers, point out the cognates.

Word	Part of Speech	Definition
agriculture	noun	farming
harvest	verb	pick crops
mild	adjective	not very hot or very cold
climate	noun	the kind of weather that a particular region has

Ask students what kinds of <u>agriculture</u> is common in California. Ask: *What time of year are different crops <u>harvested</u>?* Explain that most parts of California have a <u>mild</u> <u>climate</u> (not too hot and not too cold) that is very good for growing crops. Ask questions to check understanding of the information.

COLLABORATE

Have students work in pairs to use the words in sentences.

Analyze the Source

Teach Academic Vocabulary Write the chart below on the board. Say each word aloud and have students repeat it. For Spanish speakers, point out the cognates.

Word	Part of Speech	Definition
successful	adjective	achieving a goal
majority	verb	the largest part of something
geographic	adjective	related to the scientific study of the Earth's surface, climate, and people
ideal	adjective	perfect

Say: *California is a very special place. The state's* <u>successful</u> *farms have produced a* <u>majority</u> *of the country's fruits and vegetables. California's* <u>geographic</u> *location and climate make it* <u>ideal</u> *for growing things.*

 COLLABORATE Have students work in pairs to complete the Leveled Support activities.

Agriculture in the Central Valley

Unpack the Text Write the following sentence on the board and read it aloud:

This region is ideal for agriculture because of its fertile land and mild climate.

Explain that this sentence tells us about the Central Valley. Say: *The word* ideal *means "perfect."* Ask: *Why is the region perfect?* Elicit *fertile land and mild climate.* Say: *That's right; this sentence explains why this region produces much of the country's food.* Underline the word *because.* Say: *When you see the word* because *in a sentence, remember that it comes before a reason.*

 PRODUCTIVE Have students write a sentence using the word *because* to give a reason.

Build Meaning Offer language support for the following phrases:

top crops = most important crops in the region

fertile land = soil (dirt) that is good for growing crops

 PRODUCTIVE Have students try to use one of the phrases in a sentence.

ACADEMIC VOCABULARY

successful

majority

geographic

ideal

SPANISH COGNATES

mayoría

geográfico

ideal

LEVELED SUPPORT

EMERGING Have students imagine the ideal place to live, and complete these sentences:

1. The climate is _____.
2. It has a lot of _____, _____, and _____.

EXPANDING/BRIDGING Have students imagine the ideal place to live, and write a few sentences to describe it. They can talk about the climate, the geography, the food, and more.

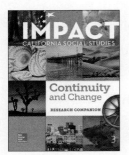

Pages 240–247

ACADEMIC VOCABULARY

process

renewable

automated

industry

SPANISH COGNATES

procesar

renovable

automatizado

industria

LEVELED SUPPORT

EMERGING Have students make a list of:

1. Things they know how to do (skills)
2. Things they know a lot about (knowledge)
3. Things they have done (experiences)

EXPANDING/BRIDGING

Have students do the *emerging* task, and then write one sentence about a skill, one about knowledge, and one about an experience.

TEXT:Leopold, Aldo. A Sand County Almanac and Sketches Here and There. Oxford, N.Y.: Oxford University Press, 1949.

Research Companion, pages 240–247

Teach Academic Vocabulary Write the chart below on the board. Say each word aloud and have students repeat it. For Spanish speakers, point out the cognates.

Word	Part of Speech	Definition
process	verb	treat raw food in order to change or preserve it
renewable	adjective	able to be replaced
automated	adjective	operated by machines or computers
industry	noun	the companies and activities that provide particular products or services

Say: *Some food companies* <u>process</u> *the foods they make. The food looks different and sometimes lasts longer. The sun is a source of* <u>renewable</u> *energy because the sun always shines! These days, many factories are* <u>automated</u>*. Machines and computers do most of the work. Tourism is a huge* <u>industry</u> *in California. Many people want to come here to visit.*

COLLABORATE
Have students use the words in their own sentences.

How Businesses Use Resources

Unpack the Text Write the following sentence on the board and read it aloud:

People who work in the factory operate the machines.

Make sure students understand all the words in the sentence. Draw a box around the clause *who work in the factory*. Say: *This sentence gives us information about people who operate machines.* Ask: *What is this sentence about?* Point out that the subject of the sentence is the word *People*. Say: *Notice the words I underlined. These words are called an* adjective clause*. The clause modifies, or tells more about, the subject—people. It explains which people the sentence is talking about.*

PRODUCTIVE
Have students work in pairs to write a sentence with a dependent clause using the sentence frame:

Students who _____ go to my school.

Unlock the Primary Source Read Leopold's words aloud and explain them:

Original Text	Contemporary English
"When we see land as a community to which we belong, we may begin to use it with love and respect." —Aldo Leopold	If we could look at the land in the same way that we look at the people we live with, then we would treat it with the respect it deserves.

Build Meaning Offer language support for the following phrases:

cannot live without = unable to survive without

human capital = a person's skills, knowledge, and experience

Possessives Remind students that when we write about something that belongs to someone, we use a punctuation mark called an apostrophe. Draw the chart below on the board. Write the noun *Camilla* on the board. Say: *Camilla has a restaurant.* Model forming the possessive by adding an apostrophe to the word *Camilla.* Then say: *People love to eat at Camilla's restaurant.* Have the students repeat the words *Camilla's restaurant* after you. Say: *The restaurant belongs to Camilla.* Explain that when a noun ends in *s*, like in the name *Carlos*, we usually put an apostrophe after the *s* but don't put another *s* after it.

GRAPHIC ORGANIZER

Noun	Belongs to	Possessive
restaurant	Camilla	Camilla's restaurant
dog	Neighbor	neighbor's dog
market	Farmer	Farmer's market
friend	Carlos	Carlos' friend

COLLABORATE
Distribute the graphic organizer to students. Write the words in the first two columns on the board and have students complete the third column in their charts.

Inquiry Journal, pages 248–249

Report Your Findings

Demonstrate Understanding Review the **Report Your Findings** task with students.

Think About It Review key vocabulary words. Have students think about the types of businesses found in California.

Write About It Place students in pairs. Have students write a paragraph describing a business they think is affected by the environment. Have students give reasons for their answers.

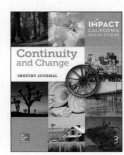
Pages 248–249

Provide assistance writing as needed.

EMERGING	The business _____ is affected by the environment when _____.
EXPANDING/ BRIDGING	I think the business _____ is affected _____ because _____.

Talk About It Have students discuss their opinions and reasons with a classmate who choose a different business. Ask: *Do you agree or disagree with your partner's opinion?*

COLLABORATE
Foster interaction by having students of different proficiencies discuss their ideas as they answer the Lesson Question.

Connect to the Essential Question Have students explain how businesses in their community use resources to help people meet their needs.

How Have Goods and Services Changed Over Time?

CONTENT OBJECTIVES

- Examine how goods and services in California have changed over time.
- Understand how California's communities use goods and services.
- Describe how community economics have developed.

LANGUAGE OBJECTIVES

- Identify prepositional phrases.
- Identify adverbs.
- Recognize compound words.

Pages 250–255

SPANISH COGNATE

jornada

petróleo

Inquiry Journal, pages 250–255

Introduce the Lesson

Access Prior Knowledge Before presenting the Lesson Outcomes, read the Lesson Question and find out what students already know about how goods and services have changed over time. Make sure students understand the meaning of *goods* and *services*. Ask: *What products do we buy now that we didn't buy many years ago? Are there services that used to exist, but don't anymore? Or services that we have now, but didn't have a long time ago?*

Teach Content Vocabulary Write the chart below on the board. Say each word aloud and have students repeat it. For Spanish speakers, point out the cognates.

Word	Part of Speech	Definition
journey	noun	a long trip
petroleum	noun	a dark, thick oil from under the ground that is made into fuels
film	noun	movie

Ask: *Have you ever taken a long journey? Where did you travel?* Explain that *petroleum* is a natural resource that businesses use to produce goods and services. Ask: *Where in California do people make a lot of films?* Elicit *Los Angeles* or *Hollywood*.

COLLABORATE Have students work in pairs to use the words in sentences.

Analyze the Source

Teach Academic Vocabulary Write the chart below on the board. Say each word aloud and have students repeat it. For Spanish speakers, point out the cognate.

Word	Part of Speech	Definition
item	noun	a thing
variety	noun	many different kinds of things or people
available	adjective	able to be obtained or gotten

Hold up a pencil and a piece of paper. Say: *In English, we have several words that we can use to name these. We can call them objects, things, or <u>items</u>. When you go into a store, you can choose from a <u>variety</u> of items that are <u>available</u>.* Ask questions to check understanding of the information.

COLLABORATE Have students work in pairs to do the Leveled Support activities.

Build Meaning Offer language support for the following phrases:

one kind of = one type of

not easy to get = hard to find

many different kinds = a variety of types

PRODUCTIVE Have students try to use one of the phrases in a sentence.

Shopping Long Ago and Today

Unpack the Text Write the following sentence on the board and read it aloud:

> It was hard to bring a special item from another country to a small store in California.

Explain that prepositional phrases give information about time, location, position, and direction. Say: *This sentence contains several prepositional phrases that tell us* where. Circle *from, to,* and *in.* Have students say the prepositions aloud. Underline the phrase *in California.* Say: *In this sentence, the word* in *points out which state. The first phrase,* from another country, *gives more information about the item. The second phrase,* to a small store, *tells us where the item goes.* Ask questions to check comprehension: *What was it that was hard to bring? Where was it that it was hard to bring from? Where was it that it was hard to bring to?*

PRODUCTIVE Have students write a sentence using a preposition to tell where.

ACADEMIC VOCABULARY

item

available

variety

SPANISH COGNATE

variedad

LEVELED SUPPORT

EMERGING Have students list as many items as they can think of that a grocery store nearby sells.

EXPANDING Have students write sentences with two of the words, and then read each other's sentences aloud.

BRIDGING Have students write an advertisement for a store, using at least three of the words.

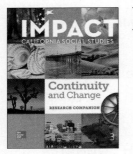

Pages 248–253

ACADEMIC VOCABULARY

technology

major

transit

region

SPANISH COGNATES

tecnología

tránsito

region

LEVELED SUPPORT

EMERGING Have students write several sentences using these frames:

I ____ quickly.
I ____ easily.

EXPANDING/BRIDGING Have students write several sentences with the adverbs *quickly* and *easily*.

Research Companion, pages 248-253

Teach Academic Vocabulary Write the chart below on the board. Say each word aloud and have students repeat it. For Spanish speakers, point out the cognates.

Word	Part of Speech	Definition
technology	noun	the practical uses of science, especially to build machines
major	adjective	important
transit	noun	transportation
region	noun	a large area of land

Ask questions to check for understanding: *What does modern <u>technology</u> help people do? Where are <u>major</u> industries located in California? What is an example of a <u>transit</u> system? What are the four main <u>regions</u> in California?*

COLLABORATE Reinforce the concept of how goods and services have changed over time. Have students name some of the goods and services in their community. Have them explain how these have changed.

Build Meaning Offer language support for the following phrases:

citrus fruits = lemons, limes, and oranges

tourism and service industries = theme parks, restaurants, and hotels

California's Railroads Over Time

Unpack the Text Write the following sentence on the board and read it aloud:

Subways and transit systems help people travel quickly and easily.

Underline the word *quickly*. Make sure students understand the meaning of the words *subways* and *transit systems*. Draw a circle around the verb *help*. Explain that the word *quickly* describes how the subways and transit systems move. Remind students that adverbs describe verbs and add information to a sentence. Say: *Adverbs are used to explain how, where, when, and why.* Ask: *How did the subways and transit systems help people travel?* Elicit *quickly and easily.* Point out many adverbs end in *-ly*.

 PRODUCTIVE Have students work in pairs to complete the Leveled Support activities.

Compound Words Remind students that compound words are two words that are put together to form one word. Draw the chart on the board. Say: *The word* shipyard *is made up of two words,* ship *and* yard. Give an example of a sentence using the compound word: *The* shipyard *launched its newest ship when it was completed.* Repeat the procedure with the following words: *farmland, grapefruit, nowhere,* and *railroad.*

Compound word	Part 1	Part 2
shipyard	ship	yard

COLLABORATE Distribute the graphic organizer to students. Have them work in pairs to find more compound words in the text and add them to the chart.

Inquiry Journal, pages 256–257

Report Your Findings

Demonstrate Understanding Review the **Report Your Findings** task with students. Remind them of the goods and services businesses in California have provided. Review the words in the Word Bank with the students. Provide assistance with vocabulary, pronunciation, and idea formation as needed.

Write About It Place students in pairs. Have students write a journal entry describing goods and services you would have used in your community 100 years ago. Provide students with writing assistance as needed.

EMERGING In our community _____. You have probably used _____. We have _____.

EXPANDING Living in our community you more than likely have _____. You might experience _____. You've probably used _____.

BRIDGING I count on my community to provide _____. You may also use as I have _____. I am dependent on _____.

Talk About It Have students share their journal entries with their partners. Discuss how goods and services have changed over time.

COLLABORATE Foster interaction by having students of different proficiencies discuss their ideas as they answer the Lesson Question.

Connect to the Essential Question Have students list what goods and services their community provides. Explain how these goods and services help people meet their needs.

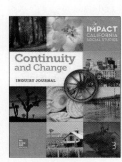

Pages 256–257

CULTIVATE MEANING and SUPPORT LANGUAGE

How Do Businesses Make Money?

CONTENT OBJECTIVES

- Examine how businesses make money.
- Understand how people make money around world.
- Describe how businesses in your community make a profit by selling goods and services.

LANGUAGE OBJECTIVES

- Identify clauses in a sentence.
- Identify prepositional phrases.
- Use contractions.

Pages 258–263

SPANISH COGNATES

secretaria

labor

TEXT:Perez, Thomas. "Justice and Identity." Washington, D.C., June 30, 2014

Inquiry Journal, pages 258–263

Introduce the Lesson

Access Prior Knowledge Before presenting the Lesson Outcomes, read the Lesson Question and find out what students already know about how businesses make money. Ask: *How does a business make money?* Ask students for examples of businesses in their community, such as a pizza restaurant. Ask: *What do they sell? What do they have to spend money on? How do they make money?*

Teach Content Vocabulary Write the chart below on the board. Say each word aloud and have students repeat it. For Spanish speakers, point out the cognates.

Word	Part of Speech	Definition
secretary	noun	an office worker or the title of a government department leader
labor	noun	work
workforce	noun	all the people who work in a particular place (city, state or country)
succeed	verb	achieve a goal

Write *secretary* on the board. Explain that in the text, *secretary* is used as a title. Say: *Thomas Perez was the <u>Secretary</u> of <u>Labor</u>. That meant he was responsible for laws that related to the <u>workforce</u> the United States.* Say: *When secretary begins with a capital letter, we know it is a job title. If it is not capitalized, then it means a person who works in an office. A secretary does a variety of jobs to help a business <u>succeed</u>.* Explain that we often say *administrative assistant* instead of *secretary*.

Unlock the Primary Source Read the words of Thomas Perez aloud. Have students use their fingers to follow along in the original text, matching words and phrases.

Thomas Perez's Words	What His Words Mean
"Our workforce and our entire economy are strongest when we embrace diversity to its fullest, and that means opening doors of opportunity to everyone and recognizing that the American Dream excludes no one."	Our economy is the strongest when everyone takes part. The American Dream is for everyone.

Analyze the Source

Teach Academic Vocabulary Write the chart below on the board. Say each word aloud and have students repeat it. For Spanish speakers, point out the cognates.

Word	Part of Speech	Definition
recognize	verb	accept that something is true
exclude	verb	leave out
improve	verb	make something or someone better
operate	verb	manage or run a company or business

Say: *We <u>recognize</u> that some industries and professions <u>exclude</u> people. So, we try to <u>improve</u> the way that those industries <u>operate</u>.* Point out that in Chapter 4, Lesson 2, students learned a different meaning of *recognize: identify from earlier experience.* In this lesson, the meaning is *accept that something is true.*

COLLABORATE Have students work in pairs to write sentences using two of the words. Then have them read each other's sentences aloud.

Build Meaning Offer language support for the following phrases:

make money = earn money

hire people = give people jobs

create jobs = make new jobs for people

opening doors = giving people new opportunities

PRODUCTIVE Have students work in pairs to do the Leveled Support activities.

The American Dream

Unpack the Text Write the following sentence on the board and read it aloud:

When people work together, it makes the business a better place to work.

Say: *This sentence explains what happens when people work together.* Underline *When people work together.* Point out that this first group of words gives more information about the main part of the sentence. Circle *it makes the business a better place to work.* Say: It *is the subject and* makes *is the verb. The business is the object.* Say: *Here is another way to write the sentence to make it easier to understand.* Write this sentence on the board:

A business is a better place to work when people work together.

PRODUCTIVE Have students write a sentence using this sentence frame:

When _____, _____.

SPANISH COGNATES

reconocer

excluir

operar

LEVELED SUPPORT

EMERGING Have students write sentences using these frames:

Now, I can make money by _____ing and _____ing. When I'm an adult, I hope to make money by _____ing.

EXPANDING/BRIDGING Have students write three sentences about ways they can make money, and then share their ideas with a partner.

Pages 254–263

ACADEMIC VOCABULARY

exist

consumer

organic

chemical

SPANISH COGNATES

existir

consumidor

orgánico

química

Research Companion, pages 254–263

Teach Academic Vocabulary Write the chart below on the board. Say each word aloud and have students repeat it. For Spanish speakers, point out the cognates.

Word	Part of Speech	Definition
exist	verb	be real
consumer	noun	a person who buys something
organic	adjective	produced without using harmful chemicals
chemical	noun	substance used to produce a reaction

Ask questions to check for understanding: *What businesses in your community do you think will <u>exist</u> in the future? What are some ways that businesses attract <u>consumers</u>? Why do farmers grow <u>organic</u> corn, without <u>chemicals</u>?* (Accept all reasonable answers.)

COLLABORATE Reinforce the concept of how businesses make their money. Have students name some businesses they think make a lot of money. Ask them to explain their reasons for their opinions.

Build Meaning Offer language support for the following phrases:

manufactured locally = made in the community

higher wages = better pay

provide a service = do something for someone

Where Goods Come From

Unpack the Text Write the following sentence on the board and read it aloud:

In the past, people made or grew most of the things they needed in their communities.

Say: *This sentence contains two prepositional phrases that begin with the same preposition, but tell us different things.* Remind students that prepositional phrases can tell us more about key words in a sentence. Underline the phrase *in the past.* Say: *Here, the word* in *points out when an action took place.* Circle *in their communities.* Say: *The second phrase,* in their communities, *tells us where they made or grew things. So when we see the word* in, *we know we need to keep reading to find out whether we're being told more about time or location.*

PRODUCTIVE Have students work in pairs to write several sentences using prepositional phrases. Have them use these sentence frames:

In the past, _____.

In our community, _____.

Contractions Remind students that a contraction is two words that have been put together. Say: *When we put two words together, we take out some of the letters. We put an apostrophe in the place of the missing letters.* Draw the chart on the board. Call on volunteers to suggest the contraction in the third column of the chart.

First Word	Second Word	Contraction
you	have	you've
let	us	let's
that	is	that's
where	is	where's

COLLABORATE Distribute copies of the graphic organizer to students. Have them work in pairs to complete the Leveled Support activities.

Inquiry Journal, pages 264–265

Report Your Findings

Demonstrate Understanding Review the **Report Your Findings** task with students. Remind them of how businesses make a profit. Review the words in the Word Bank with the students. Provide assistance with vocabulary, pronunciation, and idea formation as needed.

Write About It Place students in pairs. Have students write a paragraph explaining how businesses make a profit. Provide assistance writing as needed.

EMERGING Businesses in our community _____. You have probably used _____.

EXPANDING Businesses in our community make a profit _____. An example of a business _____. You've probably used _____.

BRIDGING One profitable businesses in my community makes a profit by _____. You may be wondering _____. If you look at _____.

Talk About It Have students share their paragraphs with their partners. Discuss how making a profit can help a business continue to meet people's needs.

COLLABORATE Foster interaction by having students of different proficiencies discuss their ideas as they answer the Lesson Question.

Connect to the Essential Question Have students explain how successful businesses help the people in their community succeed.

LEVELED SUPPORT

EMERGING Have students think of and write three more contractions.

EXPANDING/BRIDGING Have students write the words in the chart that form these contractions:

we'd, they've, I'll, wouldn't, won't

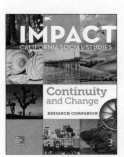

Pages 264–265

How Can People Spend Money Wisely?

CONTENT OBJECTIVES

- Examine how people choose to spend their money.
- Understand how to make good choices about spending money.
- Explain how to spend money wisely.

LANGUAGE OBJECTIVES

- Identify the linking verb *is*.
- Explore clauses in questions.
- Form past tense of irregular verbs.

Pages 266–271

SPANISH COGNATES

experiencia

propriedad

costo

TEXT: Franklin, Benjamin. Poor Richard's Almanack: by Benjamin Franklin. Waterloo, Iowa: The U.S.C. Publishing Co., 1914.

Inquiry Journal, pages 266–271

Introduce the Lesson

Access Prior Knowledge Before presenting the Lesson Outcomes, read the Lesson Question and find out what students already know about how people choose to spend money. Ask: *What are some things that people often spend money on? What do they* need *to spend money on? What do they often* want *to spend money on? What should people think about before they decide to spend money?*

Teach Content Vocabulary Write the chart below on the board. Say each word aloud and have students repeat it. For Spanish speakers, point out the cognates.

Word	Part of Speech	Definition
experience	noun	knowledge or skills you get by doing things
property	noun	things or land owned by someone
cost	noun	the amount of money you have to pay for something
allowance	noun	money given to a child each week or month

Say: *Your* experience *is all the things have you have done. Your* property *is everything you own.* Ask: *Is playing soccer property or an experience? How about a car?* Ask: *What are the* costs *of owning a car?* Elicit answers like *gas* and *repairs.* Ask: *Do you think children should have to do work at home to get an* allowance*? Why or why not?*

Unlock the Primary Source Read the words of Benjamin Franklin aloud. Have students use their fingers to follow along in the original text, matching words and phrases.

Benjamin Franklin's Words	What His Words Mean
"Beware of little expenses, a small leak will sink a great ship." —Benjamin Franklin, *Poor Richard's Almanack*	Small costs can add up to a lot of money and cause trouble later on.

Analyze the Source

Teach Academic Vocabulary Write the chart below on the board. Say each word aloud and have students repeat it.

Word	Part of Speech	Definition
beware	noun	be careful of
save	verb	keep something, usually money, to use later
wisely	adverb	in a smart, sensible way
purchase	verb	something that you bought

Say: _Beware of spending your all your money. If you save wisely, you can use your money later for something important._ Point out that _purchase_ can be a noun or a verb. When it's a noun, it means _something you bought_. When it's a verb, it means _to buy something_.

 COLLABORATE Have students work in pairs to do the Leveled Support activities.

Build Meaning Offer language support for the following phrases:

most expensive = costing the most money

best choice = the wisest decision

without thinking about it = not taking time to think about it

 PRODUCTIVE Have students try to use one of the phrases in a sentence.

Good Money Choices

Unpack the Text Write the following sentence on the board:

Is the most expensive item the best choice?

Read the sentence aloud. Ask: _What kind of sentence is this?_ Elicit _It's a question_. Circle the question mark. Say: _This sentence is a question, but it does not begin with one of the question words, such as_ Why, Where, What, _or_ When. _It begins with the helping verb_ Is. Say: _If we don't use a question word, then we start with a helping verb, like_ Is, Are, Do, Does, _or_ Did. Note that questions like this are looking for a simple answer: _Yes_ or _no_.

PRODUCTIVE Have students work in pairs to make write three or four questions that begin with _is_ or _are_ and can be answered _yes_ or _no_. Have them use the following sentence frames:

Is _____?

Yes / No.

Are _____?

Yes / No.

ACADEMIC VOCABULARY

beware

save

wisely

purchase

LEVELED SUPPORT

EMERGING Have students list three things they want to purchase.

EXPANDING/BRIDGING Have students write three reasons why it's important to save money.

IMPACT
CALIFORNIA SOCIAL STUDIES
Continuity and Change
RESEARCH COMPANION
3

Pages 264–271

ACADEMIC VOCABULARY

conduct

raise

funds

operator

SPANISH COGNATES

fondos

operario, operador

Research Companion, pages 264–271

Teach Academic Vocabulary Write the chart below on the board. Say each word aloud and have students repeat it. For Spanish speakers, point out the cognates.

Word	Part of Speech	Definition
conduct	verb	organize and do an activity
raise	verb	collect money
funds	noun	money for a specific purpose
operator	noun	someone who controls a machine or vehicle

Say: *Imagine that you want to* conduct *a fundraiser to help victims of an earthquake.* Ask: *What are some ways you can* raise funds? Say: *For example, you could have a bake sale. What are some other ideas?* Say: *A forklift* operator *often works in a factory. The operator uses a forklift to move heavy boxes.*

COLLABORATE Reinforce the concept of how people can spend their money wisely. Have students explain why people should spend money for needs before wants.

Build Meaning Offer language support for the following phrases in the text:

doing chores = doing jobs at home, such as cleaning

unexpected expense = something that you have to spend money on that you hadn't planned to spend

Making Economic Choices

Unpack the Text Write the following sentence on the board and read it aloud:

Knowing that there is only so much money to spend helps people make decisions on what to buy.

Check that students understand all the vocabulary. Clarify the meanings as needed. Circle the clause *Knowing that there is only so much money to spend.* Say: *Sometimes, sentences start with clauses like this. They act as the subject of the sentence.* Ask: *What is the verb or action word?* Elicit that *helps* is the verb. Tell students the next part explains what will happen if you know *there is only so much money to spend.* The words *people make decisions* is telling us the result. Say: *Let's write the sentence as two sentences. We can take out some words to make it easier to understand.*

We know there is only so much money to spend.

This helps us decide what to buy.

PRODUCTIVE Have students work in pairs to rewrite the following sentence as two sentences to make it easier to understand.

We use money because it is an easy way to exchange things of equal value.

Past Tense Verbs (Irregular) Check that students understand the meaning of *past* and *present*. Review past and present tense. Remind students that many past tense verbs are formed by adding *-d* or *-ed*, but others, called irregular verbs, have a different form in the past tense. Give the example of *was* and *were*. Draw the chart below on the board. Name some irregular action words, such as *make, sell, hold,* and *spend*. Model forming the past tense of each.

Present Tense	Past Tense
make	made
sell	sold
hold	held
spend	spent

 COLLABORATE Distribute copies of the graphic organizer to students. Have students work in pairs to complete the Leveled Support activities.

Inquiry Journal, pages 272–281

Report Your Findings

Demonstrate Understanding Review the **Report Your Findings** task with students. Remind them of how people spend money wisely. Have students make a list of questions that will help them decide what to buy and when to buy it. Review the words in the Word Bank with students. Provide assistance with vocabulary, pronunciation, and idea formation as needed.

Write About It Place students in pairs. Have students define a want and a need. Have them write the questions they should consider before they buy something. Have them use details from the text in their responses. Provide assistance writing as needed.

EMERGING Before I buy something I consider _____.

EXPANDING/ BRIDGING An important thing to ask myself before I spend money is _____.

Talk About It Have students compare their lists with their partners. Discuss which questions you both think are the most important.

 COLLABORATE Foster interaction by having students of different proficiencies discuss their ideas as they answer the Lesson Question.

Take Action

Project Wrap-Up Review the **Tips for Presenting** with students and check for understanding. Explain any unfamiliar terms and vocabulary. Provide support as needed as students complete the **Project Rubric** and **Project Reflection**.

GRAPHIC ORGANIZER

LEVELED SUPPORT

EMERGING Have students find three irregular past tense verbs in the text.

EXPANDING Have students think of three more irregular past tense verbs and write a sentence with each.

BRIDGING Have students write a paragraph about what they did yesterday, using at least three irregular past tense verbs.

 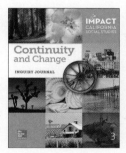

Pages 272–281

Grades K-8

IMPACT
LANGUAGE TRANSFERS
HANDBOOK

Table of Contents

Introduction to Linguistics

Each human language is a complex system of sounds, words, and grammar that enables speakers of that language to communicate with each other. All people know at least one language, whether spoken or signed. Linguistics is the study of language and includes the sounds, vocabulary, and rules.

Language can be seen to have five major components.

Phonology – the study of the sounds and the sound system of a language

Morphology – the study of the formation and structure of words

Syntax – the study of how words are combined into sentences

Semantics – the study of the ways that language conveys meaning

Pragmatics – the study of language use and how language can be affected by context

There are about 5,000 languages in the world and linguists have learned that they share many of the same sounds and properties. As students acquire English, they need more than just the vocabulary and the grammar. They need explicit instruction and practice to build skills in each of the major components of language and to communicate effectively Depending on the student's native language, the challenges that are encountered can vary from one student to another.

All languages have vowels and consonants, many of which transfer to English. Consonants are formed by obstructing the passage of air from the lungs, through the vocal cords, and out the mouth. They are described by the following characteristics: voicing, place of articulation, and manner of articulation. Vowels are sounds that are produced with an open continuous stream of air. They are described by the following characteristics: position of the tongue, tension of the vocal tract, and position of the lips.

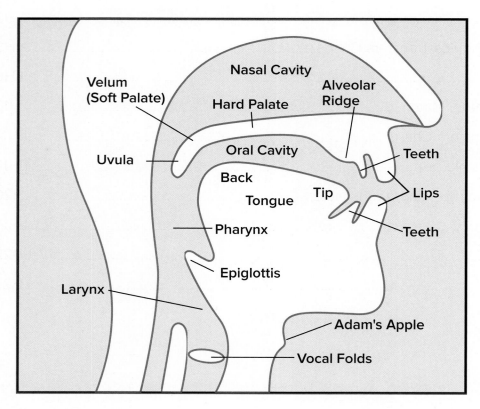

The human vocal tract makes the sounds of speech.

ERL/McGraw-Hill Education

Speaking English

English can be pronounced differently by different speakers. This is most notable when thinking about the differences between British English and American English. There are also variations in American English. For example, consider the variations between the English spoken in the Southern United States, in Boston, in Brooklyn, and so on.

In American English, there are approximately 48 sounds, but only 26 letters with which to represent them. Because there is no direct correspondence between the sounds and the letters, English learners do not have a clear pattern to guide them as they learn the pronunciation of English words.

The International Phonetic Alphabet (IPA) was created to represent all sounds used in all languages, independent of the language's orthographic rules and conventions. The chart that follows shows the IPA symbols used to represent the consonants and vowels of American English. Many language learner dictionaries use the IPA.

Consonants

IPA	Example
p	pit
b	bit
m	man
w	win
f	fun
v	very
θ	thing
ð	there
t	time
d	dime
n	name
g	goat
ŋ	king

IPA	Example
s	soy
z	zeal
ɾ	butter
l	loop
r	red
ʃ	shallow
ʒ	vision
tʃ	chirp
dʒ	joy
j	you
k	kite
h	hope

Vowels

IPA	Example
i	beat
ɪ	bit
e	bait
ɛ	bet
æ	bat
u	boot
ʊ	could
o	boat
ɔ	law
ɑ	hot
ə	about
ʌ	cut
ɝ	bird
ɑʊ	house
ɔɪ	boy
ɑɪ	bite

Language Transfer

All languages share the same fundamentals. Some languages, though, have different places and/or manners of articulation; some languages have varying numbers of vowels. Arabic is the language of many countries and has 28 consonants and 8 vowels and diphthongs. English, on the other hand, has 24 consonants and 22 vowels and diphthongs. Not surprisingly, English learners will have difficulty distinguishing between some of the words they hear (ship/sheep) and difficulty pronouncing the words correctly.

Grammar and word order can also prove challenging. English follows the pattern Subject + Verb + Object. Some languages do not. English requires that an adjective precede the noun modified. Other languages, such as Spanish and Hmong, require that adjectives follow the noun modified. The use of articles varies widely. Spanish, for example, uses definite articles more frequently than English. Arabic has a definite article, but its use is not identical to English. There are no modal verbs in Arabic and the verb be does not exist in the present tense.

It should not be surprising that students whose first language does not use the Latin alphabet will have significant difficulties. These students need much more time to learn to read in English and must not only know the Latin alphabet, but in some cases, the direction in which to read. Further, many languages make no distinction between the upper and lower cases and the rules for punctuation are much looser than in English.

The charts on the following pages highlight specific phonemes and grammatical structures that may cause problems for speakers of particular languages.

Monkey Business Images/Shutterstock.com

How to Use the Sound and Phonics Transfers Charts

To read and speak fluently in English, English learners need to master a wide range of phonemic awareness, phonics, and word study skills. The Sound and Phonics Transfer Charts are designed to help you anticipate and understand possible student errors in pronouncing or perceiving English sounds.

one
HIGHLIGHT TRANSFERRABLE SKILLS

If the phonics skill transfers from a particular native language to English and that language group is the only one being taught, state that during the lesson. In most lessons an English learner feature will indicate which sounds do and do not transfer in specific languages.

two
PRETEACH NON-TRANSFERRABLE SKILLS

Prior to teaching a phonics lesson, check the chart to determine if the sound and/or spelling transfers from a student's native language into English. If it does not, preteach the sound and spelling during Small Group time. Focus on articulation, using the backs of the small Sound-Spelling Cards, and the minimal contrast activities provided.

three
PROVIDE ADDITIONAL PRACTICE AND TIME

If the skill does NOT transfer from the student's native language into English, the student will require more time and practice mastering the sound and spellings. Continue to review the phonics skill during Small Group time in upcoming weeks until the student has mastered it. Use decodable texts to provide oral and silent reading practice. Remember not to treat accents as "errors" but as new sounds in transition.

Sound Transfers

This chart indicates areas in which a positive or approximate transfer of sounds occurs for English learners from their native languages into English. It also shows which sounds students can produce even when there are no equivalents in the native language.

IPA	Sound Transfers	Spanish	Cantonese	Vietnamese
Consonants				
b	/b/ as in **b**at	✔		●
k	/k/ as in cat, **k**itten, pe**ck**	✔	✔	●
d	/d/ as in **d**og	✔	●	●
f	/f/ as in **f**arm	✔	✔	✔
g	/g/ as in **g**irl	✔	●	
h	/h/ as in **h**am	✔	✔	✔
dʒ	/j/ as in **j**et, pa**ge**, led**ge**			
l	/l/ as in **l**ion	✔	✔	✔
m	/m/ as in **m**at	✔	✔	✔
n	/n/ as in **n**ight	✔	✔	✔
p	/p/ as in **p**en	✔	✔	✔
kw	/kw/ as in **qu**een	✔	●	✔
r	/r/ as in **r**ope	●		
s	/s/ as in **s**ink, **c**ity	✔	✔	✔
t	/t/ as in **t**on	✔	●	●
v	/v/ as in **v**ine	★		✔
w	/w/ as in **w**ind	✔	✔	
ks	/ks/ as in si**x**	✔		
y	/y/ as in **y**ak	✔	✔	✔
z	/z/ as in **z**ebra	★		✔
Digraphs				
tʃ	/ch/ as in **ch**eek, pat**ch**	✔		●
ʃ	/sh/ as in **sh**adow		●	✔
ʍ	/hw/ as in **wh**istle		●	
θ	/th/ as in pa**th**	●		●
ð	/TH/ as in **th**at	●		
ŋ	/ng/ as in sti**ng**	✔	✔	✔

Key:
- ✓ positive transfer
- ● approximate
- ★ No equivalent, but students can produce the sound.

Hmong	Korean	Tagalog	Arabic
	●	✓	✓
✓	●	●	✓
✓	●	✓	✓
✓			✓
●	●		✓
✓	✓	✓	✓
	●		
✓			✓
✓	✓		✓
✓	✓	✓	✓
●	✓	✓	✓
	✓		✓
	●	●	✓
✓	✓	✓	✓
●	✓	✓	✓
✓			✓
	✓		✓
	✓		✓
✓	✓	✓	✓
★			✓
✓	✓	✓	
✓	✓		✓
	✓	✓	
			✓
✓			✓
✓	✓	●	✓

Key:

✔ positive transfer

● approximate

★ No equivalent, but students can produce the sound.

IPA	Sound Transfers	Spanish	Cantonese	Vietnamese
Short Vowels				
æ	/a/ as in cat	●		●
ɛ	/e/ as in net	✔	●	●
ɪ	/i/ as in kid	●	●	
ɑ	/o/ as in spot	●	●	●
ʌ	/u/ as in cup	●	●	✔
Long Vowels				
e	/ā/ as in lake, nail, bay	✔	●	●
i	/ē/ as in bee, meat, cranky	✔	●	✔
ɑɪ	/ī/ as in kite, tie, light, dry	✔	●	✔
o	/ō/ as in home, road, row	✔	●	●
u	/ū/ as in dune, fruit, blue	✔	●	✔
ju	/yü / as in mule, cue	✔	●	
r-Controlled Vowels				
ɑr	/är/ as in far	●	●	
ɔr	/ôr/ as in corn	●	●	
ɜ	/ûr/ as in stern, bird, suburb	●	●	
ɛr	/âr/ as in air, bear			
ɪr	/îr/ as in deer, ear			
Variant Vowels				
ɔɪ	/oi/ as in boil, toy	✔	●	●
ɑʊ	/ou/ as in loud, down	✔	●	✔
ɔ	/ô/ as in law	●	✔	✔
ɔ	/ô/ as in laundry	●	●	✔
ɑl	/ôl/ as in salt, call	●	●	
u	/oo/ as in moon, drew	✔	●	●
ʊ	/ŏo/ as in look		●	●
ə	/ə/ as in askew			●

Hmong	Korean	Tagalog	Arabic
✓	✓	✓	
	✓		✓
	✓	✓	✓
●	●	✓	✓
	✓	●	✓
●	✓	●	
✓	✓	●	●
✓	✓	●	
	✓	✓	
✓	✓	✓	●
	✓		✓
			●
	✓	✓	
●	✓	✓	✓
●	●	●	
●	●	✓	
	●	✓	
✓	✓	✓	
	●	✓	
	✓		
	✓		

Phonics Transfers:
Sound-Symbol Match

Sound-Symbol Match	Spanish	Cantonese	Vietnamese
Consonants			
/b/ as in **b**at	✓		✓
/k/ as in **c**at	✓		✓
/k/ as in **k**itten	✓		✓
/k/ as in pe**ck**			
/d/ as in **d**og	✓		✓
/f/ as in **f**arm	✓		
/g/ as in **g**irl	✓		✓
/h/ as in **h**am			✓
/j/ as in **j**et, pa**ge**, led**ge**			
/l/ as in **l**ion	✓		✓
/m/ as in **m**at	✓		✓
/n/ as in **n**ight	✓		✓
/p/ as in **p**en	✓		✓
/kw/ as in **qu**een			✓
/r/ as in **r**ope			
/s/ as in **s**ink, **c**ity	✓		✓
/t/ as in **t**on	✓		✓
/v/ as in **v**ine	✓		✓
/w/ as in **w**ind	✓		
/ks/ as in si**x**	✓		
/y/ as in **y**ak	✓		
/z/ as in **z**ebra			
Digraphs			
/ch/ as in **ch**eek, pat**ch**	✓		
/sh/ as in **sh**adow			
/hw/ as in **wh**istle			
/th/ as in pa**th**			✓
/TH/ as in **th**at			
/ng/ as in sti**ng**	✓		✓
Short Vowels			
/a/ as in cat			✓
/e/ as in net	✓		✓
/i/ as in kid			
/o/ as in spot			✓
/u/ as in cup			

Hmong	Korean	Tagalog	Arabic
		✔	
✔		✔	
✔		✔	
✔			
		✔	
✔			
✔		✔	
✔		✔	
✔		✔	
✔		✔	
		✔	
✔		✔	
✔			
		✔	
✔		✔	
		✔	
✔			
		✔	
		✔	
✔			

Sound-Symbol Match	Spanish	Cantonese	Vietnamese
Long Vowels			
/ā/ as in l**a**ke	✔		
/ā/ as in n**ai**l			
/ā/ as in b**ay**	✔		
/ē/ as in b**ee**	✔		
/ē/ as in m**ea**t			
/ē/ as in crank**y**			
/ī/ as in k**i**te, t**ie**, l**igh**t, dr**y**	✔		
/ō/ as in h**o**me, r**oa**d, r**ow**	✔		
/ū/ as in d**u**ne			✔
/ū/ as in fr**ui**t, bl**ue**			
/yū/ as in m**u**le, c**ue**			
r-Controlled Vowels			
/är/ as in f**ar**	✔		
/ôr/ as in c**or**n	✔		
/ûr/ as in st**er**n	✔		
/ûr/ as in b**ir**d, sub**ur**b			
/âr/ as in **air**, b**ear**			
/îr/ as in d**eer**, **ear**			
Variant Vowels			
/oi/ as in b**oi**l	✔		✔
/oi/ as in t**oy**	✔		
/ou/ as in l**ou**d			
/ou/ as in d**ow**n			
/ô/ as in l**aw**			
/ô/ as in l**au**ndry			
/ôl/ as in s**al**t	✔		
/ôl/ as in c**all**	✔		
/oo/ as in m**oo**n, dr**ew**			
/o˘o/ as in l**oo**k			
/ə/ as in **a**skew			

Hmong	Korean	Tagalog	Arabic
		✔	
✔			
		✔	
		✔	

How to Use the Grammar Transfers Charts

English language grammar differs widely from that of many other languages. For example, a student's primary language may use a different word order than English does, may not use parts of speech in the same way, or may use different verb tenses. The Grammar Transfers Charts are designed to help you anticipate possible transfer errors in speaking and writing in standard English. With all grammar exercises, the emphasis is on oral communication, both as a speaker and listener.

one

HIGHLIGHT TRANSFERRABLE SKILLS

If the grammar skill transfers from the student's native language to English and that language group is the only one being taught, state that it transfers during the first few sessions. In many lessons, an English learner feature will indicate which skills do and do not transfer.

two

PRETEACH NON-TRANSFERRABLE SKILLS

Prior to teaching a grammar lesson, check the chart to determine if the skill transfers from the student's native language into English. If it does not, preteach the skill during Small Group time. Provide sentence frames and ample structured and unstructured opportunities to use the skill in spoken English. Students need to talk, talk, and talk some more to master these skills. Use songs, games, rhymes, short skits, and poems to supplement the frames.

three

PROVIDE ADDITIONAL PRACTICE AND TIME

If the skill does NOT transfer from the student's native language into English, the student will require more time and practice mastering it. Continue to review the skill during Small Group time. Use the additional resources, such as the grammar lessons in the **Language Development Kits** (K-6), in upcoming weeks. Include the skill in the reviewing that you do for the class as a whole so English learners do not feel singled out when you do class work.

four
USE CONTRASTIVE ANALYSIS

When you are teaching a single language group, tell students when a skill does not transfer and include contrastive analysis work to make the students aware of how to correct their speaking and writing for standard English. For example, when a student uses an incorrect grammatical form, write the student's sentence on a work board. Then write the correct English form underneath. Explain the difference between the student's native language and English. Have the student correct several other sentences using this skill.

five
INCREASE WRITING AND SPEAKING OPPORTUNITIES

Increase the amount of structured writing and speaking opportunities for students needing work on specific grammatical forms. Sentence starters and paragraph frames such as those found in the lessons, are ideal for both written and oral exercises. Plays, short poems, focused conversations, and song lyrics provide other ways to practice speaking.

six
FOCUS ON MEANING

Always focus on the meaning of sentences in all exercises. As students improve and fine-tune their English speaking and writing skills, work with students on basic comprehension of spoken and written English.

Grammar Transfers:
Grammatical Form

This chart can be used to address common mistakes that some English learners make when they transfer grammatical forms from their native languages into English.

Grammatical Form	Transfer Mistakes in English	Native Language	Cause of Difficulty
Nouns			
Plural Marker -s	**Forgets plural marker -s** *I have 3 sister.*	Cantonese, Hmong, Korean, Vietnamese, Arabic, Spanish	Native language does not use a plural marker or students do not transfer.
Countable and Uncountable Nouns	**Confuses countable and uncountable nouns** *the homeworks* or *the informations*	Tagalog, Spanish	Countable and uncountable nouns are different in English and native language.
Possessives	**Uses prepositions to describe possessives** *the book of my brother* as opposed to *my brother's book*	Hmong, Spanish, Vietnamese, Arabic	Possession is often described using a prepositional phrase.
	Avoids using 's *dog of my father* as opposed to *my father's dog*	Vietnamese	A noun follows the object in the native language.
Articles			
	Consistently omits articles *He has book. They want dog not cat.*	Cantonese, Hmong, Korean, Vietnamese, Arabic, Tagalog	There is no article in the native language or no difference between *the* and *a*.
	Overuses articles *The English is difficult. The soccer is popular in the Europe.*	Hmong, Spanish, Arabic, Tagalog, Cantonese, Korean	Some languages use articles that are omitted in English.
a/an	**Mistakes one for a/an** *She is one nurse.*	Hmong, Vietnamese, Korean, Arabic, Tagalog, Cantonese	The native language either does not use articles or uses articles differently; or *one* and *a/an* are the same words.
Pronouns			
Gender- Specific Pronouns	**Uses pronouns with the inappropriate gender** *He is my sister.*	Cantonese, Hmong, Korean, Spanish, Tagalog, Vietnamese	The third person pronoun in the native language is gender free, or the personal pronoun is omitted.
	Uses inappropriate gender, particularly with neutral nouns *The day is sunny. She is beautiful.*	Spanish, Vietnamese, Hmong	Nouns have feminine or masculine gender in the native language, and the gender may be carried

			over into English.
Object Pronouns	**Confuses subject and object pronouns** *Her talks to me.*	Cantonese, Hmong	The same pronoun form is used for subject and object in the native language.
	Omits object pronouns *That girl is very rude, so nobody likes.*	Korean, Vietnamese	The native language does not use direct objects.
Pronoun and Number Agreement	**Uses the wrong number for pronouns** *I saw many red birds. It was pretty.*	Cantonese, Korean, Arabic	The native language does not require number agreement.
Subject Pronouns	**Omits subject pronouns** *Mom isn't home. Is at work.*	Korean, Spanish, Vietnamese	Subject pronouns may be dropped because in the native language the verb ending gives information about the number and/or gender.
Pronouns in Clauses	**Omits pronouns in clauses** *If don't do homework, they will not learn.*	Cantonese, Vietnamese, Tagalog	The native language does not need a subject in the subordinate clause.
Pronouns and Nouns	**Overuses pronouns with nouns** *This school, it is very good.*	Vietnamese	This is popular in speech in some languages. The speaker mentions a topic, then makes a comment about it.
	Avoids pronouns and repeats nouns *Carla visits her sister every Sunday, and Carla makes a meal.*	Korean, Vietnamese	In the native language, the speaker repeats nouns and does not use pronouns.
Pronoun *one*	**Omits the pronoun one** *I saw two dogs, and I like the small.*	Spanish, Vietnamese	Adjectives can stand alone in the native language, but English requires a noun or *one*.
Possessive Forms	**Confuses possessive forms** *The book is my.*	Cantonese, Hmong, Vietnamese	Cantonese and Hmong speakers tend to omit the final *n* sound, which may create confusion between *my* and *mine*.

Verbs

Present Tense	**Omits -s in present tense, third person agreement** *He like pizza.*	Cantonese, Hmong, Korean, Vietnamese, Arabic, Tagalog	Subject-verb agreement is not used in the native language.
Irregular Verbs	**Has problems with irregular subject-verb agreement** *Tom and Sue has a new car.*	Cantonese, Hmong, Korean, Arabic, Tagalog	Verbs' forms do not change to show the number of the subject in the native language.

Grammar Transfers

Inflectional Endings	**Omits tense markers** I _study_ English yesterday.	Cantonese, Hmong, Korean, Vietnamese	The native language does not use inflectional endings to change verb tense.
Present and Future Tenses	**Incorrectly uses the present tense for the future tense** I go next week.	Cantonese, Korean, Spanish, Arabic, Tagalog	The native language may use the present tense to imply the future tense.
Negative Statements	**Omits helping verbs in negative statements** Sue no coming to school.	Cantonese, Korean, Spanish, Arabic	The native language does not use helping verbs in negative statements.
Present-Perfect Tense	**Avoids the present-perfect tense** Marcos live here for three months.	Vietnamese, Arabic, Korean, Hmong	The native language does not use the present-perfect verb form.
Past-Continuous Tense	**Uses the past-continuous tense for recurring action in the past** When I was young, I was talking a lot.	Korean, Spanish, Arabic, Hmong	In the native language, the past-continuous tense is used but in English the expression used to or the simple past tense is used.
Main Verb	**Omits the main verb** Talk in class not good.	Cantonese, Hmong	Cantonese does not require an infinitive marker when using a verb as a noun. Speakers may confuse the infinitive for the main verb.
Main Verbs in Clauses	**Uses two or more main verbs in one clause without any connectors** I took a book went studied at the library.	Hmong, Tagalog	In Hmong, verbs can be used consecutively without conjunctions or punctuation.
Linking Verbs	**Omits the linking verb** He hungry.	Cantonese, Hmong, Vietnamese	In some languages, _be_ is implied in the adjective form. In other languages, the concept is expressed with a verb.
Helping Verb in Passive Voice	**Omits the helping verb in the passive voice** The homework done.	Cantonese, Vietnamese, Arabic, Hmong	In Cantonese and Vietnamese, the passive voice does not require a helping verb.

Verbs

Passive Voice	**Avoids the passive voice** They speak English here. One speaks English here. English is spoken here.	Hmong, Vietnamese	Is expressed in verbs of experience in Vietnamese.
Transitive Verbs	**Confuses transitive and intransitive verbs** The child broke. The child broke _the plate._	Cantonese, Korean, Spanish, Arabic, Hmong	Verbs that require a direct object differ between English and the native language.

Phrasal Verbs	Confuses related phrasal verbs *I ate at the apple.* *I ate up the apple.*	Korean, Spanish, Arabic	Phrasal verbs are not used in the native language, and there is often confusion over their meaning.
Have and be	Uses have instead of be *I have thirst.* *He has right.*	Spanish, Arabic	Spanish and English have different uses for *have* and *be*.

Adjectives

Word Order	Places adjectives after nouns *I saw a car red.*	Hmong, Spanish, Vietnamese, Abaric	Nouns often precede adjectives in the native language.
	Consistently places adjectives after nouns *This is a lesson new.*	Cantonese, Korean, Spanish, Hmong	Adjectives always follow nouns in the native language.
-er and -est Endings	Avoids -er and -est endings *I am more old than you.*	Hmong, Korean, Spanish, Tagalog	The native language shows comparative and superlative forms with separate words.
-ing and -ed Endings	Confuses -ing and -ed forms *Math is bored.*	Cantonese, Korean, Spanish	Adjectives in the native language do not have active and passive meanings.

Adverbs

Adjectives and Adverbs	Uses an adjective where an adverb is needed *Talk quiet.*	Hmong, Cantonese	Adverbs modify verbs and adjectives in Cantonese.
Word Order	Places adverbs before verbs *He quickly ran.* *He ran quickly.*	Cantonese, Korean, Hmong	Adverbs usually come before verbs in the native language, and this tendency is carried over into English.

Prepositions

	Omits prepositions *I like come school.*	Cantonese, Hmong	Prepositions are not used the same way they are in English.

Cognate Knowledge and Comprehension

Cognates are words that have similar spellings, meanings, and sometimes similar pronunciations across two languages. They make up one third to one half of the words in languages that share cognates with English, for example, Spanish, French, and Portuguese. Cognates are often useful in promoting comprehension for students whose native language has a Latin base. For example, using "calculate the mass/volume ratio" may be easier for some students to understand than "figure out the mass/volume ratio" as "calcular" is a Spanish cognate.

Studies indicate that—under some circumstances—English learners whose first language shares cognates with English are able to draw on first language knowledge to figure out the meanings of cognates in their second language.

- Knowledge of cognates may provide Spanish-speaking bilingual students with an advantage in learning academic language (Lubliner & Grishan, 2012).

- Research documents the efficacy of Cognate Strategy Instruction (Lubliner & Grishan, 2012; Moran, 2011).

- Cognates are plentiful in Academic Language (Coxhead, 2000; Hiebert & Lubliner, 2011).

- Using cognates during instruction is an important strategy for English learners whose first language shares cognates with English (Kamil & Hiebert, 2005).

- Students use their first-language knowledge in inferring the meaning of unknown second-language words that are cognates (August, 2009; August, Branum-Martin, Cardenas-Hagan, & Francis, 2009; Carlo et al., 2004).

- Once taught, the transparency of cognate pairs may enhance bilingual students' reading comprehension (August & Shanahan, 2009).

- Students who are not literate, but are orally proficient in Spanish, might benefit from instruction in cognate awareness.

- Instruction can facilitate English learners' ability to draw on their first language knowledge (August & Shanahan, 2006).

While in most cases cognate knowledge is helpful, in some cases it may result in English learners inferring the wrong meaning of unknown words, as when words are false cognates (amigos falsos). They look and sound alike in both languages but do not have any of the same meanings, or they share some meanings but not the meaning required in a particular context (Garcia, 1991).

Cognates Strategy Instruction

Help students whose first language shares cognates with English draw on their first language knowledge by teaching how to use cognate knowledge:

- Explain what cognates are: cognates are words that look similar, sound similar, and share meanings across some languages.

- Explain that many words have multiple meanings and sometimes cognates share one meaning but not others.

- Explain that sometimes words look and/or sound alike but are not cognates. Pie is an example. It means "foot" in Spanish but "a type of pastry" in English.

- Model differences and similarities, in sounds and letters, for example: *mysterious* and *misterioso*.

- Ask students whose first language shares cognate status with English to pronounce the pairs and note similarities and differences in sounds.

- Ask students to find letters in the pairs that are similar.

- Give students the opportunity to find cognates in authentic text.

- Ask students to check to see if the meaning of the word in their first language makes sense in the English sentence.

- Check a dictionary to confirm.

Ariel Skelley/Blend Images

Sample Teacher Lesson

Teacher Instructions: Cognates make up one-half to one-third of the words in languages that share cognates with English (e.g., Spanish, French, Portuguese). Some of the cognates may be technical terms and therefore unknown to students in both languages *(hypothesis/hipótesis)*. The Spanish word in a cognate pair tends to be an easier, more well-known word to Spanish speakers than the English word is to English speakers. Cognates can help students figure out the meaning of academic English words they don't know and it will help them remember the words they have already learned.

Teach students how to use cognates.

- Show cognate word pairs and images on an interactive whiteboard or screen *(liberty/libertad)*.

- Explain that these words are cognates. They are in two different languages, but they look similar, they sound similar, and they mean approximately the same thing.

- Model differences and similarities for *liberty* and *libertad:*

- They have many of the same letters, but some letters are different.

- Ask a native Spanish speaker to say *liberty* and compare the sounds in *libertad*. The consonants are similar, but some of the vowels and the ending sound different.

- Partner-talk: *Look at the words* liberty/libertad *and* disagreeable/desagradable. *Which letters are the same? Do the words sound similar enough that you would recognize they may be related?*

- Explain to students that when they encounter a word they don't know, but it has lots of the same letters and sounds the same, it may be a cognate, and they should check to see if the meaning of the word in their native language makes sense in the English sentence that includes the cognate. It is always important to then check a dictionary.

- Explain to students that words can have multiple meanings. Not all meanings of a cognate will be the same in both languages. Explain to students that they also need to watch out for false cognates, which are words that sound the same and/or are spelled the same, but have different meanings *(pie/pie)*.

- Give students an opportunity to practice.

- Have students use the table in the student chart to practice checking words for cognate status.

- For each word pair, have students rate whether the words *look* the same and/or *sound* the same on a scale of 1 to 3 (3 is perfect or near perfect correspondence).

- Students should use a dictionary or the sample sentence to test the meaning of each English word and indicate whether the words in the pair share the same *meaning*.

- Students should indicate whether the pair is a cognate pair based on their ratings.

Sample Student Practice

COLLABORATE

Student Practice: Cognates are words in two different languages that look similar, sound similar, and mean approximately, or almost the same thing. Work with a partner. Fill in the chart below:

- Give a number from 1-3 to each pair of words based on sound and appearance (how they look). The number 1 means they are not at all alike, or similar. The number 3 means that they are almost the same.

- Look up the words in a dictionary or try using the Spanish word in the English example sentence to see whether it makes sense. If the words mean the same or almost the same, write "yes" in the Same Meaning column. Write "no" if they do not.

- In the last column, write "yes" if you think the words are cognates and write "no" if you think they are not.

	English	Spanish	Sound (1,2,3)	Appearance (1,2,3)	Same meaning? (yes/no)	Are they cognates? (yes/no)
1.	**body**	**boda**	**2**	**1**	**No**	**No**
The elephant has a very large <u>body</u>.						
2.	*color*	*color*	2	3	Yes	Yes
My favorite <u>color</u> is green.						
3.	**appeared**	**parecía**				
Laura <u>appeared</u> tired and ready to go to sleep.						
4.	ill	enfermo				
Lucia is <u>ill</u> with a fever and a cough.						
5.	**expression**	**expresión**				
He had a happy <u>expression</u> on his face.						
6.	**morning**	**mañana**				
The sun rises in the <u>morning</u>.						
7.	**native**	**nativo**				
Raul is a <u>native</u> of Argentina.						
8.	**government**	**gobierno**				
The city <u>government</u> built a public park.						
9.	**real**	**real**				
My sandals are made of <u>real</u> leather.						
10.	**actual**	**actual**				
The <u>actual</u> cost of the movie tickets was more than I thought.						

Diane August and Erin Haynes, Center for English Language Learners, American Institutes for Research.

IMPACT
CALIFORNIA SOCIAL STUDIES

CALIFORNIA
ENGLISH LANGUAGE
DEVELOPMENT STANDARDS

GRADE 3

Mc
Graw
Hill
Education

STANDARD	DESCRIPTOR	CITATIONS
PART I: Interacting in Meaningful Ways		
A. Collaborative		
ELD.PI.3.1	**EXCHANGING INFORMATION AND IDEAS**	
	EMERGING	
	Contribute to conversations and express ideas by asking and answering *yes-no* and *wh-* questions and responding using short phrases.	4–7, 8–11, 12–15, 16–19, 20–23, 24–27, 30–33, 34–37, 38–41, 42–45, 46–49, 50–53, 56–59, 60–63, 64–67, 68–71, 72–75, 76–79, 82–85, 86–89, 90–93, 94–97, 98–101, 102–105, 106–109, 112–115, 116–119, 120–123, 124–127
	EXPANDING	
	Contribute to class, group, and partner discussions, including sustained dialogue, by following turn-taking rules, asking relevant questions, affirming others, and adding relevant information.	4–7, 8–11, 12–15, 16–19, 20–23, 24–27, 30–33, 34–37, 38–41, 42–45, 46–49, 50–53, 56–59, 60–63, 64–67, 68–71, 72–75, 76–79, 82–85, 86–89, 90–93, 94–97, 98–101, 102–105, 106–109, 112–115, 116–119, 120–123, 124–127
	BRIDGING	
	Contribute to class, group, and partner discussions, including sustained dialogue, by following turn-taking rules, asking relevant questions, affirming others, adding relevant information, building on responses, and providing useful feedback.	4–7, 8–11, 12–15, 16–19, 20–23, 24–27, 30–33, 34–37, 38–41, 42–45, 46–49, 50–53, 56–59, 60–63, 64–67, 68–71, 72–75, 76–79, 82–85, 86–89, 90–93, 94–97, 98–101, 102–105, 106–109, 112–115, 116–119, 120–123, 124–127
ELD.PI.3.2	**INTERACTING VIA WRITTEN ENGLISH**	
	EMERGING	
	Collaborate with peers on joint writing projects of short informational and literary texts, using technology where appropriate for publishing, graphics, and the like.	7, 15, 19, 20, 27, 31, 32, 43–45, 53, 59, 63, 69, 71, 79, 83, 85, 87, 91, 93, 95, 101, 105, 107, 113, 115, 117, 119, 121, 123, 127
	EXPANDING	
	Collaborate with peers on joint writing projects of longer informational and literary texts, using technology where appropriate for publishing, graphics, and the like.	7, 15, 19, 20, 27, 31, 32, 43–45, 53, 59, 63, 69, 71, 79, 83, 85, 87, 91, 93, 95, 101, 105, 107, 113, 115, 117, 119, 121, 123, 127
	BRIDGING	
	Collaborate with peers on joint writing projects of a variety of longer informational and literary texts, using technology where appropriate for publishing, graphics, and the like.	7, 15, 19, 20, 27, 31, 32, 43–45, 53, 59, 63, 69, 71, 79, 83, 85, 87, 91, 93, 95, 101, 105, 107, 113, 115, 117, 119, 121, 123, 127

ELD.PI.3.3	OFFERING OPINIONS	
	EMERGING	
	Offer opinions and negotiate with others in conversations using basic learned phrases (e.g., *I think . . .*), as well as open responses in order to gain and/or hold the floor.	7, 11, 59, 85, 89, 109, 115
	EXPANDING	
	Offer opinions and negotiate with others in conversations using an expanded set of learned phrases (e.g., *I agree with X, and . . .*), as well as open responses in order to gain and/or hold the floor, provide counterarguments, and the like.	7, 11, 59, 85, 89, 109, 115
	BRIDGING	
	Offer opinions and negotiate with others in conversations using a variety of learned phrases (e.g., *That's a good idea, but . . .*), as well as open responses in order to gain and/or hold the floor, provide counterarguments, elaborate on an idea, and the like.	7, 11, 59, 85, 89, 109, 115
ELD.PI.3.4	ADAPTING LANGUAGE CHOICES	
	EMERGING	
	Recognize that language choices (e.g., vocabulary) vary according to social setting (e.g., playground versus classroom), with substantial support from peers or adults.	25
	EXPANDING	
	Adjust language choices (e.g., vocabulary, use of dialogue, and the like) according to purpose (e.g., persuading, entertaining), social setting, and audience (e.g., peers versus adults), with moderate support from peers or adults.	25
	BRIDGING	
	Adjust language choices according to purpose (e.g., persuading, entertaining), task, and audience (e.g., peer-to-peer versus peer-to-teacher), with light support from peers or adults.	25
B. Interpretive		
ELD.PI.3.5	LISTENING ACTIVELY	
	EMERGING	
	Demonstrate active listening to read-alouds and oral presentations by asking and answering basic questions, with prompting and substantial support.	4–7, 8–11, 12–15, 16–19, 20–23, 24–27, 30–33, 34–37, 38–41, 42–45, 46–49, 50–53, 56–59, 60–63, 64–67, 68–71, 72–75, 76–79, 82–85, 86–89, 90–92, 94–97, 98–101, 102–105, 106–109, 112–115, 116–119, 120–123, 124–127
	EXPANDING	
	Demonstrate active listening to read-alouds and oral presentations by asking and answering detailed questions, with occasional prompting and moderate support.	4–7, 8–11, 12–15, 16–19, 20–23, 24–27, 30–33, 34–37, 38–41, 42–45, 46–49, 50–53, 56–59, 60–63, 64–67, 68–71, 72–75, 76–79, 82–85, 86–89, 90–92, 94–97, 98–101, 102–105, 106–109, 112–115, 116–119, 120–123, 124–127

ELD.PI.3.6	BRIDGING	
	Demonstrate active listening to read-alouds and oral presentations by asking and answering detailed questions, with minimal prompting and light support.	4–7, 8–11, 12–15, 16–19, 20–23, 24–27, 30–33, 34–37, 38–41, 42–45, 46–49, 50–53, 56–59, 60–63, 64–67, 68–71, 72–75, 76–79, 82–85, 86–89, 90–92, 94–97, 98–101, 102–105, 106–109, 112–115, 116–119, 120–123, 124–127

ELD.PI.3.6 READING/VIEWING CLOSELY

EMERGING

Describe ideas, phenomena (e.g., insect metamorphosis), and text elements (e.g., main idea, characters, setting) based on understanding of a select set of grade-level texts and viewing of multimedia, with substantial support.	4–7, 8–11, 12–15, 16–19, 20–23, 24–27, 30–33, 34–37, 38–41, 42–45, 46–49, 50–53, 56–59, 60–63, 64–67, 68–71, 72–75, 76–79, 82–85, 86–89, 90–92, 94–97, 98–101, 102–105, 106–109, 112–115, 116–119, 120–123, 124–127

EXPANDING

Describe ideas, phenomena (e.g., how cows digest food), and text elements (e.g., main idea, characters, events) in greater detail based on understanding of a variety of grade-level texts and viewing of multimedia, with moderate support.	4–7, 8–11, 12–15, 16–19, 20–23, 24–27, 30–33, 34–37, 38–41, 42–45, 46–49, 50–53, 56–59, 60–63, 64–67, 68–71, 72–75, 76–79, 82–85, 86–89, 90–92, 94–97, 98–101, 102–105, 106–109, 112–115, 116–119, 120–123, 124–127

BRIDGING

Describe ideas, phenomena (e.g., volcanic eruptions), and text elements (e.g., central message, character traits, major events) using key details based on understanding of a variety of grade-level texts and viewing of multimedia, with light support.	4–7, 8–11, 12–15, 16–19, 20–23, 24–27, 30–33, 34–37, 38–41, 42–45, 46–49, 50–53, 56–59, 60–63, 64–67, 68–71, 72–75, 76–79, 82–85, 86–89, 90–92, 94–97, 98–101, 102–105, 106–109, 112–115, 116–119, 120–123, 124–127

ELD.PI.3.7 EVALUATING LANGUAGE CHOICES

EMERGING

Describe the language writers or speakers use to support an opinion or present an idea (e.g., by identifying the phrases or words in the text that provide evidence), with prompting and substantial support.	7, 87, 95

EXPANDING

Describe the specific language writers or speakers use to present or support an idea (e.g., the specific vocabulary or phrasing used to provide evidence), with prompting and moderate support.	7, 87, 95

BRIDGING

Describe how well writers or speakers use specific language resources to support an opinion or present an idea (e.g., whether the vocabulary or phrasing used to provide evidence is strong enough), with light support.	7, 87, 95

ELD.PI.3.8	ANALYZING LANGUAGE CHOICES	
	EMERGING	
	Distinguish how different words produce different effects on the audience (e.g., describing a character as *happy* versus *sad*).	20–23, 32, 45, 53, 87
	EXPANDING	
	Distinguish how different words with similar meanings (e.g., describing a character as *happy* versus *ecstatic*) produce shades of meaning and different effects on the audience.	20–23, 32, 45, 53, 87
	BRIDGING	
	Distinguish how multiple different words with similar meanings (e.g., *pleased* versus *happy* versus *ecstatic, heard* versus *knew* versus *believed*) produce shades of meaning and different effects on the audience.	20–23, 32, 45, 53, 87

C. Productive

ELD.PI.3.9	PRESENTING	
	EMERGING	
	Plan and deliver very brief oral presentations (e.g., retelling a story, describing an animal, and the like).	32, 35
	EXPANDING	
	Plan and deliver brief oral presentations on a variety of topics and content areas (e.g., retelling a story, explaining a science process, and the like).	32, 35
	BRIDGING	
	Plan and deliver longer oral presentations on a variety of topics and content areas (e.g., retelling a story, explaining a science process or historical event, and the like).	32, 35
ELD.PI.3.10a	WRITING	
	EMERGING	
	Write short literary and informational texts (e.g., a description of a flashlight) collaboratively (e.g., joint construction of texts with an adult or with peers) and sometimes independently.	7, 15, 19, 20, 27, 31, 32, 43–45, 53, 59, 63, 69, 71, 79, 83, 85, 87, 91, 93, 95, 101, 105, 107, 113, 115, 117, 119, 121, 123, 127
	EXPANDING	
	Write longer literary and informational texts (e.g., an explanatory text on how flashlights work) collaboratively (e.g., joint construction of texts with an adult or with peers) and with increasing independence using appropriate text organization.	7, 15, 19, 20, 27, 31, 32, 43–45, 53, 59, 63, 69, 71, 79, 83, 85, 87, 91, 93, 95, 101, 105, 107, 113, 115, 117, 119, 121, 123, 127
	BRIDGING	
	Write longer and more detailed literary and informational texts (e.g., an explanatory text on how flashlights work) collaboratively (e.g., joint construction of texts with an adult or with peers) and independently using appropriate text organization and growing understanding of register.	7, 15, 19, 20, 27, 31, 32, 43–45, 53, 59, 63, 69, 71, 79, 83, 85, 87, 91, 93, 95, 101, 105, 107, 113, 115, 117, 119, 121, 123, 127

ELD.PI.3.10b	**EMERGING**	
	Paraphrase texts and recount experiences using key words from notes or graphic organizers.	10, 91
	EXPANDING	
	Paraphrase texts and recount experiences using complete sentences and key words from notes or graphic organizers.	10, 35, 91
	BRIDGING	
	Paraphrase texts and recount experi-ences using increasingly detailed complete sentences and key words from notes or graphic organizers.	10, 35, 91
ELD.PI.3.11	**SUPPORTING OPINIONS**	
	EMERGING	
	Support opinions by providing good reasons and some textual evidence or relevant background knowledge (e.g., referring to textual evidence or knowledge of content).	7, 11, 59, 85, 89, 109, 115
	EXPANDING	
	Support opinions by providing good reasons and increasingly detailed textual evidence (e.g., providing examples from the text) or relevant background knowledge about the content.	7, 11, 59, 85, 89, 109, 115
	BRIDGING	
	Support opinions or persuade others by providing good reasons and detailed textual evidence (e.g., specific events or graphics from text) or relevant background knowledge about the content.	7, 11, 59, 85, 89, 109, 115
ELD.PI.3.12	**EMERGING**	
	Use a select number of general academic and domain-specific words to add detail (e.g., adding the word *dangerous* to describe a place, using the word *habitat* when describing animal behavior) while speaking and writing.	5, 6, 10, 11, 12, 14, 16–19, 22, 23, 24, 37, 38, 40, 85, 97, 114, 118, 119
	EXPANDING	
	Use a growing number of general academic and domain-specific words in order to add detail, create an effect (e.g., using the word *suddenly* to signal a change), or create shades of meaning (e.g., *scurry* versus *dash*) while speaking and writing.	5, 6, 10, 11, 12, 14, 16–19, 22, 23, 24, 36, 37, 38, 40, 85, 97, 111, 114, 118, 119
	BRIDGING	
	Use a wide variety of general academic and domain-specific words, synonyms, antonyms, and non-literal language to create an effect, precision, and shades of meaning while speaking and writing.	36, 97, 111

Part II: Learning About How English Works

A. Structuring Cohesive Texts

ELD.PII.3.1	UNDERSTANDING TEXT STRUCTURE	
	EMERGING	
	Apply understanding of how different text types are organized to express ideas (e.g., how a story is organized sequentially) to comprehending texts and writing basic texts.	9, 10, 13, 14, 17, 18, 21, 22, 25, 26, 31, 32, 35, 37, 39, 40, 43, 44, 47, 48, 51, 52, 57, 58, 61, 62, 65, 66, 69, 70, 73, 74, 77, 78, 83, 84, 87, 89, 91, 92, 95, 96, 99–101, 103, 104, 107, 108, 113, 114, 117, 118, 121, 122, 125, 126
	EXPANDING	
	Apply understanding of how different text types are organized to express ideas (e.g., how a story is organized sequentially with predictable stages) to comprehending texts and writing texts with increasing cohesion.	9, 10, 13, 14, 17, 18, 21, 22, 25, 26, 31, 32, 35, 37, 39, 40, 43, 44, 47, 48, 51, 52, 57, 58, 61, 62, 65, 66, 69, 70, 73, 74, 77, 78, 83, 84, 87, 89, 91, 92, 95, 96, 99–101, 103, 104, 107, 108, 113, 114, 117, 118, 121, 122, 125, 126
	BRIDGING	
	Apply understanding of how different text types are organized to express ideas (e.g., how a story is organized sequentially with predictable stages versus how opinion/arguments are structured logically, grouping related ideas) to comprehending texts and writing cohesive texts.	9, 10, 13, 14, 17, 18, 21, 22, 25, 26, 31, 32, 35, 37, 39, 40, 43, 44, 47, 48, 51, 52, 57, 58, 61, 62, 65, 66, 69, 70, 73, 74, 77, 78, 83, 84, 87, 89, 91, 92, 95, 96, 99–101, 103, 104, 107, 108, 113, 114, 117, 118, 121, 122, 125, 126
ELD.PII.3.2a	UNDERSTANDING COHESION	
	EMERGING	
	Apply basic understanding of language resources that refer the reader back or forward in text (e.g., how pronouns refer back to nouns in text) to comprehending texts and writing basic texts.	6, 9, 15, 19, 20, 22, 23, 25, 31, 36, 39, 43, 44, 47, 65, 84, 92, 96, 99, 103, 113, 121, 125
	EXPANDING	
	Apply growing understanding of language resources that refer the reader back or forward in text (e.g., how pronouns refer back to nouns in text) to comprehending texts and writing texts with increasing cohesion.	6, 9, 15, 19, 20, 22, 23, 25, 31, 36, 39, 43, 44, 47, 65, 84, 92, 96, 99, 103, 113, 121, 125
	BRIDGING	
	Apply increasing understanding of language resources that refer the reader back or forward in text (e.g., how pronouns or synonyms refer back to nouns in text) to comprehending and writing cohesive texts.	6, 9, 15, 19, 20, 22, 23, 25, 31, 36, 39, 43, 44, 47, 65, 84, 92, 96, 99, 103, 113, 121, 125
ELD.PII.3.2b	**EMERGING**	
	Apply basic understanding of how ideas, events, or reasons are linked throughout a text using everyday connecting words or phrases (e.g., *then, next*) to comprehending texts and writing basic texts.	22, 25, 36, 40, 51, 69, 84, 99
	EXPANDING	
	Apply growing understanding of how ideas, events, or reasons are linked throughout a text using a variety of connecting words or phrases (e.g., *at the beginning/end, first/next*) to comprehending texts and writing texts with increasing cohesion.	22, 25, 36, 40, 51, 69, 84, 99

	BRIDGING	
	Apply increasing understanding of how ideas, events, or reasons are linked throughout a text using an increasing variety of connecting and transitional words or phrases (e.g., *for example, afterward, first/next/last*) to comprehending texts and writing cohesive texts.	22, 25, 36, 40, 51, 69, 84, 99

B. Expanding and Enriching Ideas

ELD.PII.3.3	**USING VERBS AND VERB PHRASES**	
	EMERGING	
	Use frequently used verbs, different verb types (e.g., *doing, saying, being/having, thinking/feeling*), and verb tenses appropriate to the text type and discipline to convey time (e.g., simple past for recounting an experience).	39, 108
	EXPANDING	
	Use a growing number of verb types (e.g., *doing, saying, being/having, thinking/feeling*) and verb tenses appropriate to the text type and discipline to convey time (e.g., simple past for retelling, simple present for a science description).	39, 108
	BRIDGING	
	Use a variety of verb types (e.g., *doing, saying, being/having, thinking/feeling*) and verb tenses appropriate to the text type and discipline to convey time (e.g., simple present for a science description, simple future to predict).	39, 108
ELD.PII.3.4	**USING NOUNS AND NOUN PHRASES**	
	EMERGING	
	Expand noun phrases in simple ways (e.g., adding an adjective to a noun) in order to enrich the meaning of sentences and add details about ideas, people, things, and the like.	57, 65, 91
	EXPANDING	
	Expand noun phrases in a growing number of ways (e.g., adding comparative/superlative adjectives to nouns) in order to enrich the meaning of sentences and add details about ideas, people, things, and the like.	57, 65, 91
	BRIDGING	
	Expand noun phrases in a variety of ways (e.g., adding comparative/superlative adjectives to noun phrases, simple clause embedding) in order to enrich the meaning of sentences and add details about ideas, people, things, and the like.	57, 65, 91
ELD.PII.3.5	**MODIFYING TO ADD DETAILS**	
	EMERGING	
	Expand sentences with adverbials (e.g., adverbs, adverb phrases, prepositional phrases) to provide details (e.g., time, manner, place, cause, and the like) about a familiar activity or process (e.g., They walked *to the soccer field*).	47, 55, 88, 107, 109, 117, 118, 122
	EXPANDING	
	Expand sentences with adverbials (e.g., adverbs, adverb phrases, prepositional phrases) to provide details (e.g., time, manner, place, cause, and the like) about a familiar or new activity or process (e.g., They worked *quietly;* they ran *across the soccer field*).	47, 55, 88, 107, 109, 117, 118, 122

	BRIDGING	
	Expand sentences with adverbials (e.g., adverbs, adverb phrases, prepositional phrases) to provide details (e.g., time, manner, place, cause, and the like) about a range of familiar and new activities or processes (e.g., They worked *quietly all night in their room*).	11, 47, 55, 88, 107, 109, 117, 118, 122

C. Connecting and Condensing Ideas

ELD.PII.3.6	EXPANDING	
	Combine clauses in an increasing variety of ways (e.g., creating compound and complex sentences) to make connections between and join ideas, for example, to express cause/effect (e.g., *The deer ran because the mountain lion came*) or to make a concession (e.g., *She studied all night even though she wasn't feeling well*).	9
	BRIDGING	
	Combine clauses in a wide variety of ways (e.g., creating compound and complex sentences) to make connections between and join ideas, for example, to express cause/effect (e.g., *The deer ran because the mountain lion approached them*), to make a concession (e.g., *She studied all night even though she wasn't feeling well*), or to link two ideas that happen at the same time (e.g., *The cubs played while their mother hunted*).	9
ELD.PII.3.7	CONDENSING IDEAS	
	EMERGING	
	Condense clauses in simple ways (e.g., changing: *It's green. It's red.* → *It's green and red*) to create precise and detailed sentences in shared language activities guided by the teacher and sometimes independently.	91
	EXPANDING	
	Condense clauses in a growing number of ways (e.g., through embedded clauses as in, *It's a plant. It's found in the rain forest.* → *It's a green and red plant that's found in the tropical rain forest*) to create precise and detailed sentences.	77, 114
	BRIDGING	
	Condense clauses in a variety of ways (e.g., through embedded clauses and other condensing as in, *It's a plant. It's green and red. It's found in the tropical rain forest.* → *It's a green and red plant that's found in the tropical rain forest*) to create precise and detailed sentences.	77, 114